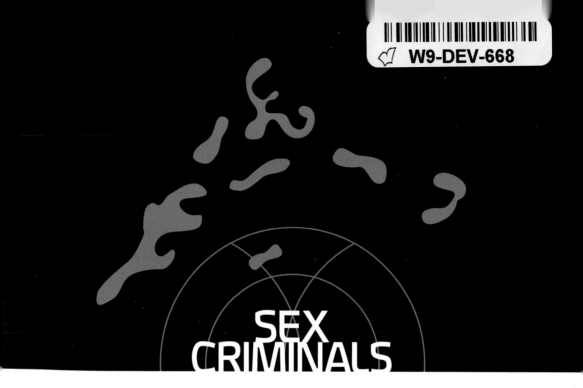

SEX CRIMINALS

SIX CRIMINALS

MATT FRACTION
CHIP ZDARSKY

THOMAS K
EDITING

ERIKA SCHNATZ
PRODUCTION

TURNER LOBEY
MANAGING EDITOR

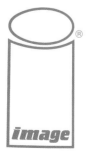

IMAGE COMICS, INC. • **Todd McFarlane:** President • **Jim Valentino:** Vice President • **Marc Silvestri:** Chief Executive Officer • **Erik Larsen:** Chief Financial Officer • **Robert Kirkman:** Chief Operating Officer • **Eric Stephenson:** Publisher / Chief Creative Officer • **Shanna Matuszak:** Editorial Coordinator • **Marla Eizik:** Talent Liaison • **Nicole Lapalme:** Controller • **Leanna Caunter:** Accounting Analyst • **Sue Korpela:** Accounting & HR Manager • **Jeff Boison:** Director of Sales & Publishing Planning • **Dirk Wood:** Director of International Sales & Licensing • **Alex Cox:** Director of Direct Market & Speciality Sales • **Chloe Ramos-Peterson:** Book Market & Library Sales Manager • **Emilio Bautista:** Digital Sales Coordinator • **Kat Salazar:** Director of PR & Marketing • **Drew Fitzgerald:** Marketing Content Associate • **Heather Doornink:** Production Director • **Drew Gill:** Art Director • **Hilary DiLoreto:** Print Manager • **Tricia Ramos:** Traffic Manager • **Erika Schnatz:** Senior Production Artist • **Ryan Brewer:** Production Artist • **Deanna Phelps:** Production Artist • **IMAGECOMICS.COM**

I don't care. Anyone but Chip. You can just fill out whatever. I just—I give up. Y'know? I don't care. I've gotten to the point where I just don't care.

MATT

To Matt. I know I've joked around a lot in these dedications over the years, but you're truly my favourite person, the one who makes me better, who pushes me to reach my potential. You're funny, brilliant and kind. I honestly don't know what I would do without you in my life. Thank you for having me along on this amazing ride. I love you.

CHIP

P.S. You're a solid 7/10.

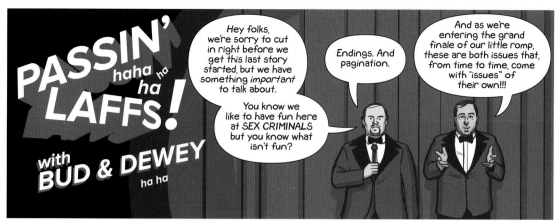

PASSIN' haha ha ha LAFFS!

with BUD & DEWEY ha ha

Hey folks, we're sorry to cut in right before we get this last story started, but we have something *important* to talk about.

You know we like to have fun here at *SEX CRIMINALS* but you know what isn't fun?

Endings. And pagination.

And as we're entering the grand finale of our little romp, these are both issues that, from time to time, come with "issues" of their own!!!

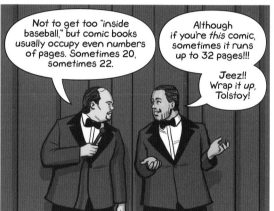

Not to get too "inside baseball," but comic books usually occupy even numbers of pages. Sometimes 20, sometimes 22.

Although if you're *this* comic, sometimes it runs up to 32 pages!!!

Jeez!! Wrap it *up*, Tolstoy!

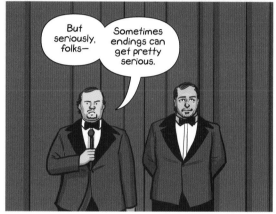

But seriously, folks—

Sometimes endings can get pretty serious.

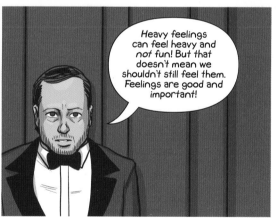

Heavy feelings can feel heavy and *not* fun! But that doesn't mean we shouldn't still feel them. Feelings are good and important!

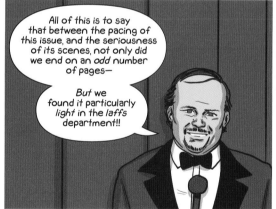

All of this is to say that between the pacing of this issue, and the seriousness of its scenes, not only did we end on an *odd* number of pages—

But we found it particularly *light* in the *laffs* department!!

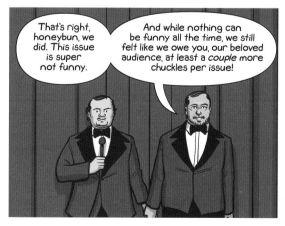

That's right, honeybun, we did. This issue is super not funny.

And while nothing can be funny all the time, we still felt like we owe you, our beloved audience, at least a *couple* more chuckles per issue!

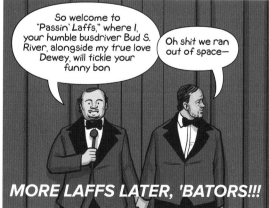

So welcome to "Passin' Laffs," where I, your humble busdriver Bud S. River, alongside my true love Dewey, will tickle your funny bon

Oh shit we ran out of space—

MORE LAFFS LATER, 'BATORS!!!

26
EVER FUCK SOMEBODY?

I'M WITH
STUNTED

♪ "What is
the fourth
dimension?" ♩

Well allow me to answer your question, ladies.
My name is Eustice K Astroturf, and these five fine brothers behind me?
They. Are the Fourth Dimension.
Now, the Fourth Dimension is more than just a band... it's more than just a sound.
Girl, the Fourth Dimension... is a viiiiiiibe.
HANDJOB RIDGE
pop. 4 fingers, 1 thumb
PEEPER'S POINT
And tonight... that vibe is strong.
And like the Chunnel—the so-called channel-tunnel connecting England to France beneath the English Channel—that vibe is never gonna be finished.
Like Major League Baseball's World Series—our vibe is reliable. Dependable. And it's always gonna happen and it's never gonna stop suddenly for a year.
And like the careers of 4 Non Blondes, Tag Team, and Rozalla, fellow musical acts that broke around the same time we have, roughly around 1992-1993—
Our vibe will *go on forever*.
So girl, that's why our song is called:
Don't forget to pull—

Fuck
—ing love this song.
Never gonna pull never gonna pull never gonna pull—
...out of the fourth dimension...
Do they mean that in a Euclidean way or more of a...
Einstein / Minkowski-y way?
What's the difference?
One's geometry. The other's ... not.
People say "Time" but that's—there's semiotic and semantic issues there.
Planck Frames—that is—
—duration. As if "future" and "past" were, like, directions.
Yes, I'm certain these one-hit R&B wonders from 1992 didn't write a song about their deep love of road-head—
—but rather the conceptual notion of rotating outside of a linear array of time and space.
That's kind of like what we do.
When we. Y'know.
We rotate out of...
"Hey, you."
EXIT
"Hey, you."
I have kind of a weird question:
Do you think she was right?

Alix, I mean.
Jesus.
About *what?*
Ha.
Everything, I guess.
Was she right about everything?
Hey you.
Hey.
Hey, so.
I got shit figured out.
We're not...
I mean...
We're not really *traumatized*, are we?

Have you ever fucked somebody, like, actively-tried-to-destroy-someone's-life fucked somebody?
I mean... how do you all see this playing out?
Us versus Badal. Versus BankCorp and all of it.
Robbing a bank? Come on. That's not this movie, the caper, the heist.
Masks and *guns* and a *getaway car.*
BADALCOR
Let alone all that *money*—not like you could ever spend it, not these days. Might as well sign your name at the scene.
So, okay, so what? We *destroy* a bank?
Sure. Which one?
There's branches. It's computers, the cloud—
SEXUAL POLICE
FOR HOLDING THE THIN BLUEBALL LINE
You can't cut the head off a monster if the monster can't be touched, and these things, these... corporate...
...entities?

The only thing that can kill them is money.
Like, god-level amounts of money. And power.
That's like fighting an idea. We're not going to hurt the bank.
So we can't rob a bank. Can't destroy the bank, all their branches, offices, ATMs, whatever—
—so all that's left to stop, to fight... is Badal.
Right?
All that's left is destroying a man's life, and I'm telling you, that's a hell of a thing. So I'm asking—
You ever really, really fuck somebody?
Because I promise you—Badal is a guy who fucks people.

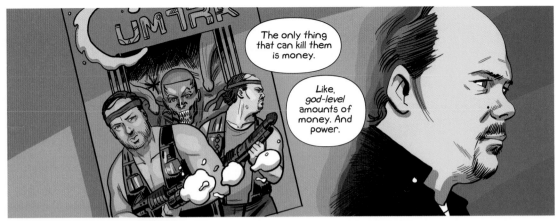

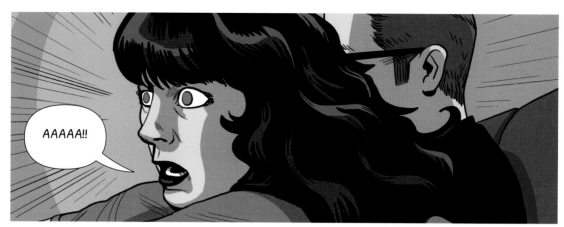

AAAAA!!

Whoa.

Dang!

Oh my *god* Dewey, I'm so sorry—

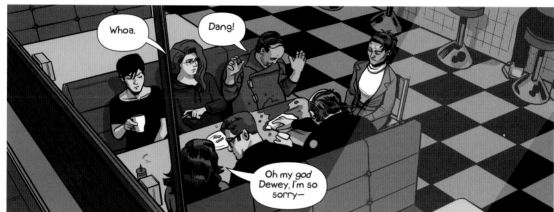

Suze? Are you okay? What the hell was that?

God, it's so embarrassing.

I'm just... sometimes I...

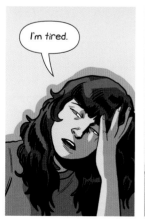

I'm tired.

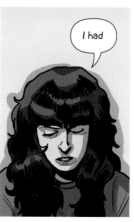

I had

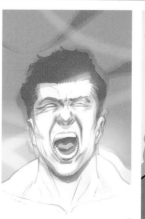

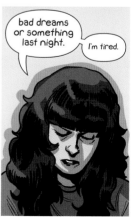

bad dreams or something last night.

I'm tired.

FUCK CAKE
CAKE IS BULLSHIT
Yes, I too often shriek and...
...flail... when I am...
...tired.
You wanna take off?
You just got here. Don't you want to eat?
Are you kidding me? Did you read the menu for this place?
I mean, I like flan but, come on.
Take a raincheck on you yelling at me, Alix? Okay?
I know the punchline anyway, you're right and we're not, I'm a dummy, blah blah.
'Night all.
Do you ever remember things?
After they happen?
Isn't that how remembering works?
(*sigh*)
You put it like that and it sounds *crazy*.

I don't like to think about myself like that, I mean.
It— I just—
I'm more than that.
I guess I never really thought about it before. Not really.
Like, I'm not a cop, I'm not a *soldier* or anything. How bad did I really
It feels like *faking* to say anything that happened to me was *traumatizing*.
I mean, bad things *happened*, but, like.
Around me.
When I think back I don't think, like—
—I don't remember ever feeling like, oh, god, *trauma*.
I felt
UNDERSTANDING COMICS:
WHAT THE FUCK DO THEY WANT FROM ME? BLOOD?
155.11 FRA
Learning To Love Again: Life After WicDiv
155.116 CAN
Death Fucking Blows
155.12 KAN
It's Okay That You're Not Okay But Frankly I'm Fine
155.125 WIL
Introvert, Outropervert
155.3 FRE
LOLITA
813.54 NAB
Why Even Bother, Really
LOSS
Unless You're Somewhere Else
155. BRE

001-099 Dicktionaries & Encyclopeenias
100-199 Feelings & Shit
LOLITA
Um, it's called the *Dewey Decimal System*, not the Alphabetical Asshole... uh.
System—
LOLITA
APPLETON 1976
APPLETON 1976
Caught you!
We're gonna have to *hire you* soon if you don't
stop
before it's too late, Kuber.
There's still
time
blahh

You okay?
Because this sounds like more than tired.
Yeah.
I am but
APPLETON 1976
Suze...
...is it happening again?
Can I, uh.
Can I ask you something?
Am I going crazy?
I think as long as you...
I think as long as you worry about going crazy...
You're probably not.

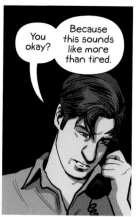

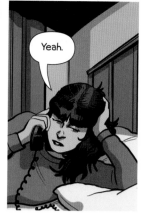

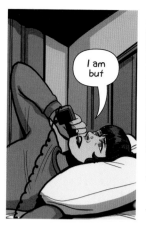

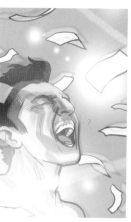

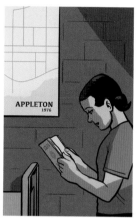

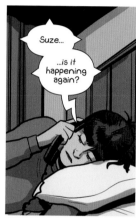

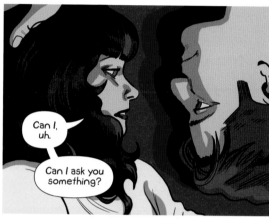

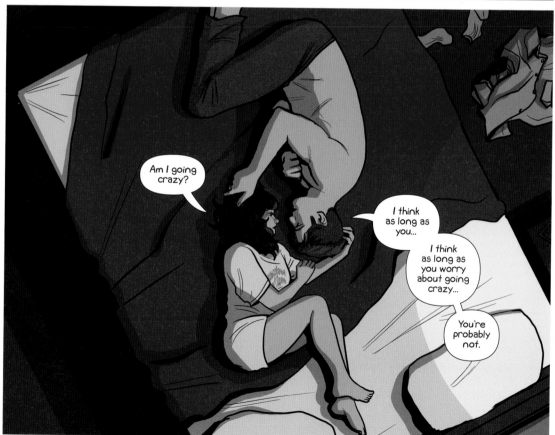

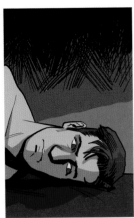

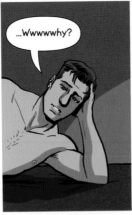

...Wwwwwhy?

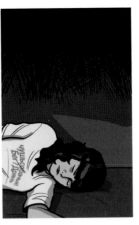

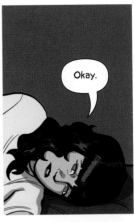

Okay.

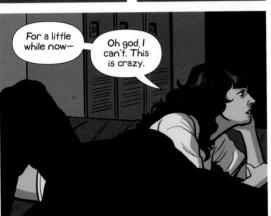

For a little while now—

Oh god, I can't. This is crazy.

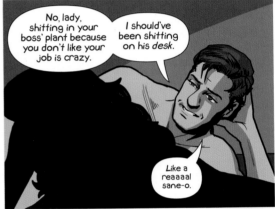

No, lady, shitting in your boss' plant because you don't like your job is crazy.

I should've been shitting on his *desk*.

Like a reaaaal sane-o.

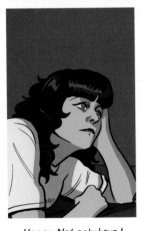

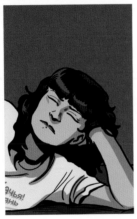

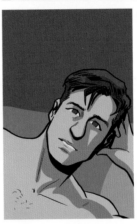

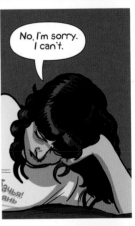

No, I'm sorry. I can't.

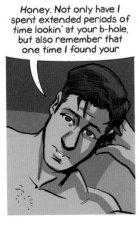

Honey. Not only have I spent extended periods of time lookin' at your b-hole, but also remember that one time I found your

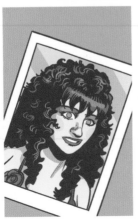

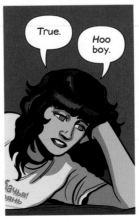

True.

Hoo boy.

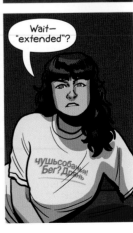

Wait— "extended"?

Well, sometimes—I mean, it's right *there*.
If you're, y'know, you're right on top of me and I'm under you and all.
чушьсобачья! Бег? Дрянь
You have a freckle.
Right there on one of the little—
If you ever die in a plane crash maybe that's how I can identif—
You know what, never mind.
Over the last few days something weird has been happening.
Like, stuff will happen—
Anything. Nothing. Totally at random, but—
But I get this, like, *flash* in my head.
And the flash is, like—
—like I remember that I already *dreamed* it was gonna happen.
But not, like, dreamed-it, dreamed it. More like I caught a glimpse of it while I was sleeping.
Thing is, though—
APPLETON
1976
—I'll remember that I already dreamed it? Like a long time ago? Or it's something
that's coming. A glimpse of something like—
like a perfume or something you smell, just for a second.
But it's not just, like—
I *felt* the future. Like I *felt* what's coming.
I think something bad is going to happen.
And I think it's our fault.
I think I've maybe been dreaming about it my whole life.

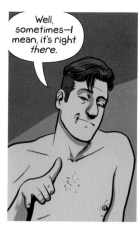

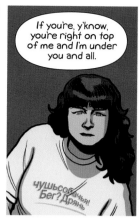

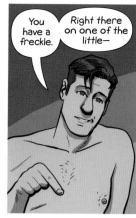

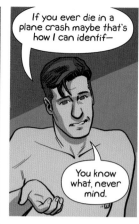

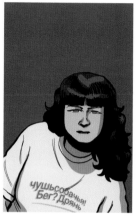

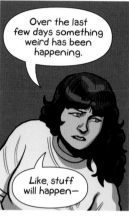

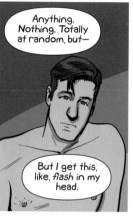

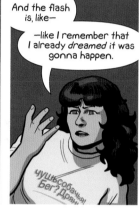

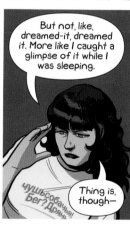

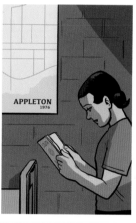

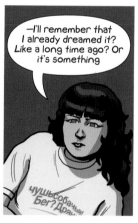

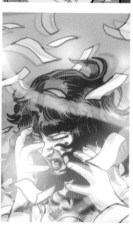

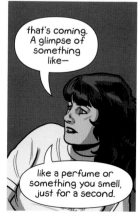

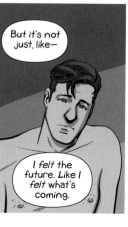

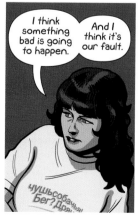

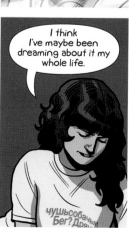

Oh, honey.
That happens to *everybody*.
Really?
чушьсобачья! Бег?Дрянь
No.
That's the craziest fucking thing I ever heard.
No, not like—
—not that *you're* crazy, that *thing* is just—
чушьсобачья! Бег?Дрянь
Suzanne, nothing matters to me but you. But us.
I don't care about the bank, Badal, Kegelface, any of it.
We never have to talk to any of those people ever again. We can leave town, shave our heads, join a circus.
S'long as it's with you. Okay?
You mean it?
Promise.
Okay.
Everything's gonna be okay in the end.
And if it's not okay—
—it's not the end.
I mean— you feel that, right?
You're feeling okay?

LO
What the hell is this?
Suzanne.
LOS
What the hell is this book?
Finding your way through grief
Why are you reading a book about loss, you wanna be sad all the time or something?
LOSS
I'm serious, Suzanne, why are you reading a book like this?
People are going to think—
—think you're crazy.
WELL?!?
kabook
SUZANNE, ANSWER ME!

...Welllll....
Because dad.
Oh, *please.*
You think *you* know about loss? You think—
You are being so *ridiculous!* We are *fine!*
You are fine!
I think maybe, uh.
Could I talk to someone? Like a doctor?
s Kitty!
God, Suzanne, you're so *funny.*
mwah
Running to the liquor store. Can I getcha anything?
This
Ha! See, you're not the *only* funny one.
NO ADULTS Allowed!
Back in ten.
Uh.
What?

"Tusk"!
It's "Tusk"!
FLEETWOOD FUCKIN' MAC
...Shit.
It's the Mac!
You don't like the Mac?
—whoa—
—why are we here?
It's just nice to have conversations in places other than that diner.
Probably more fun to draw, too.
FLEETWOOD FUCKIN' MAC
Easy there—you're looking a little wobbly.
Can, uh...
Can I ask you something? As a doctor?
Sure.

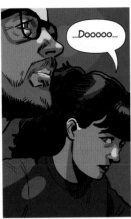
...Dooooo...

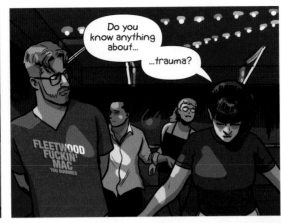
Do you know anything about...

...trauma?

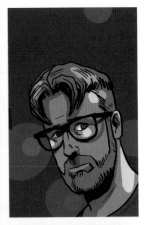

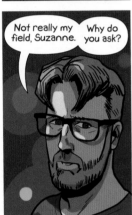
Not really my field, Suzanne.

Why do you ask?

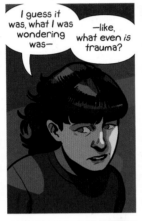
I guess it was, what I was wondering was—

—like, what even is trauma?

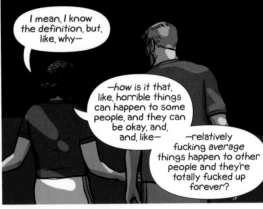
I mean, I know the definition, but, like, why—

—how is it that, like, horrible things can happen to some people, and they can be okay, and, and, like—

—relatively fucking average things happen to other people and they're totally fucked up forever?

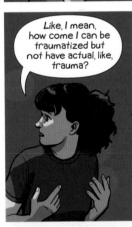
Like, I mean, how come I can be traumatized but not have actual, like, trauma?

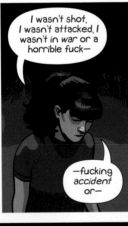
I wasn't shot, I wasn't attacked, I wasn't in war or a horrible fuck—

—fucking accident or—

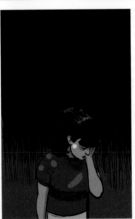

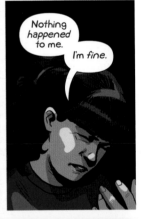
Nothing happened to me.

I'm fine.

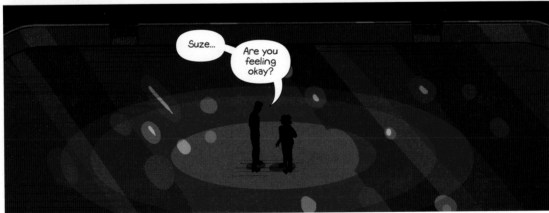
Suze...

Are you feeling okay?

Yeah.
Yeah, I'm okay.
Just tired, is all. And I miss you.

Please limit phone calls to 10 minutes maximum wait why are we saying "please" we're a prison FFS
NO ERECTIONS while talking on the phone. Erections will be punished unless that causes more erections.
I miss you too.
Three weeks, two days to go, baby. We got this.
Everything's gonna be okay.

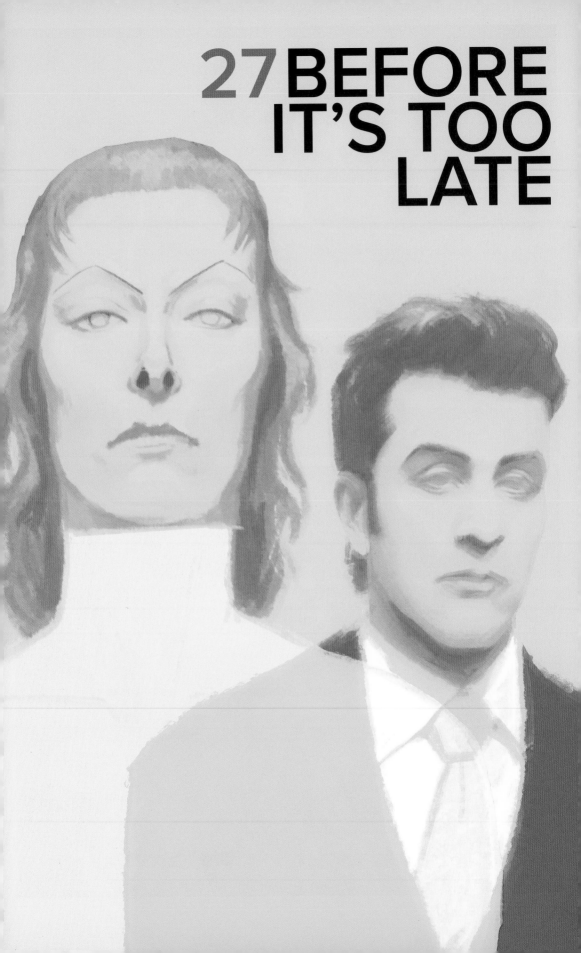

27 BEFORE IT'S TOO LATE

Quit wiggling.
Stop tickling me then—!
Look, if I don't continue the polka dots around the whole thigh it's just gonna look weird.
Mm.
SHROO
Maybe I could just draw a bikini bottom on here and save you all the time and trouble of muff-grooming.
Yeah, but you like muff-grooming.
True.
SHROOK BITCH
Hey! That's a great idea actually. Think of all the drawing surface your Wookiee-like pubes obscure.
I'm gonna grab my razor.
Turnabout's fair play, buddy — grab a razor for yourself so I can pretend I'm making out with Pinocchio.

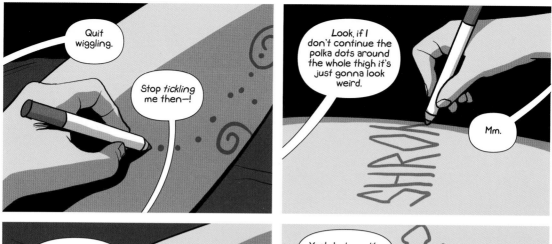

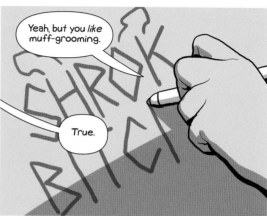

Wait, how would that work?
Would he have to lie to you the whole time or something?
"You're-a so good! I've-a never done-a this before! It's-a me, Mario!"
Grr—!
How dare you impugn my wooden puppet boyfriend.
aah okay mercy, mercy—
sigh
Okay fine.
Even lying down you are very tall.
I can tell.
Christ, look at this thing. You're like Bigfoot with alopecia or—
Hey. What's this crazy scar?
That's where I got shot.
I told you about that.

"Shot."
mm.
Shot.
Jon.
Mm?
I am going to shoot you if you don't—

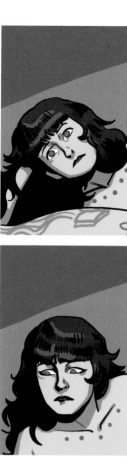

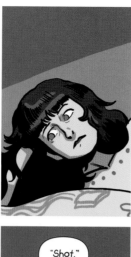

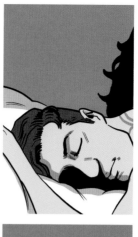

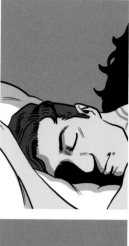

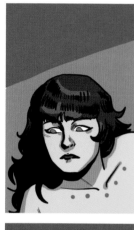

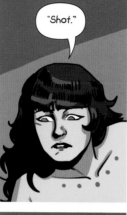

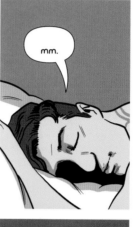

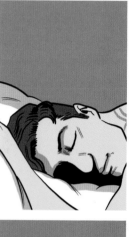

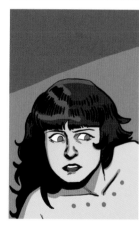

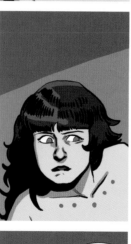

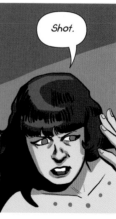

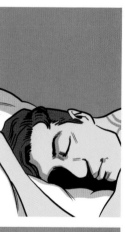

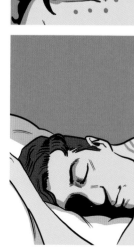

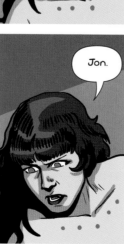

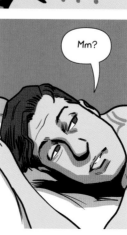

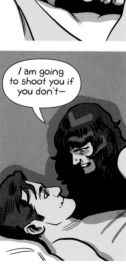

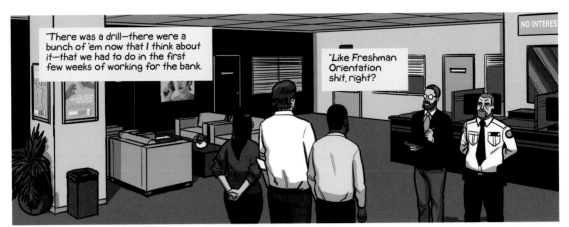

"There was a drill—there were a bunch of 'em now that I think about it—that we had to do in the first few weeks of working for the bank.

"Like Freshman Orientation shit, right?

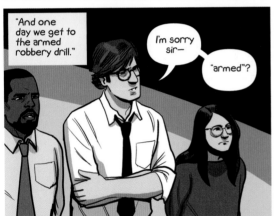

"And one day we get to the armed robbery drill."

I'm sorry sir—

"armed"?

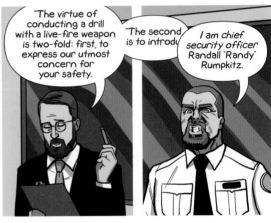

"The virtue of conducting a drill with a live-fire weapon is two-fold: first, to express our utmost concern for your safety.

"The second is to introdu—

I am chief security officer Randall "Randy" Rumpkitz.

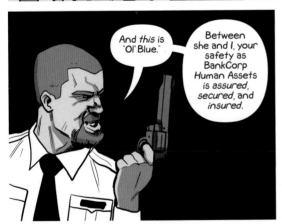

And this is "Ol' Blue."

Between she and I, your safety as BankCorp Human Assets is assured, secured, and insured.

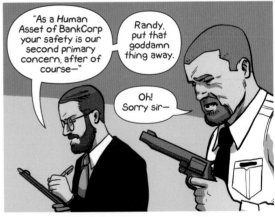

"As a Human Asset of BankCorp your safety is our second primary concern, after of course—"

Randy, put that goddamn thing away.

Oh! Sorry sir—

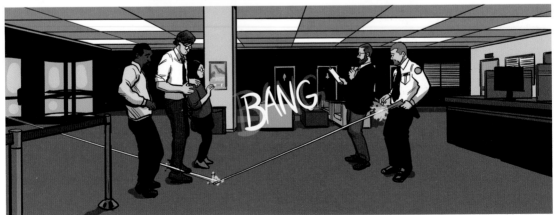

BANG

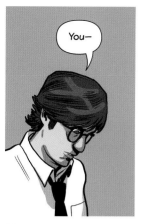
You—

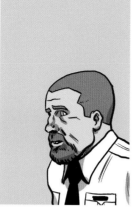

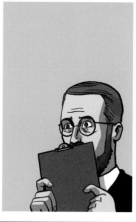

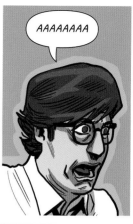
AAAAAAAA

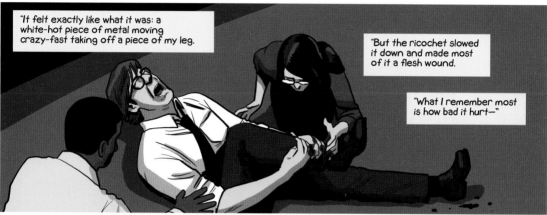
"It felt exactly like what it was: a white-hot piece of metal moving crazy-fast taking off a piece of my leg."

"But the ricochet slowed it down and made most of it a flesh wound.

"What I remember most is how bad it hurt—"

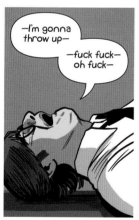
—I'm gonna throw up—

—fuck fuck— oh fuck—

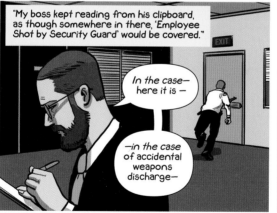
"My boss kept reading from his clipboard, as though somewhere in there, 'Employee Shot by Security Guard' would be covered."

In the case— here it is —

—in the case of accidental weapons discharge—

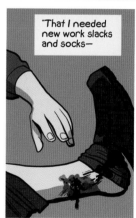
"That I needed new work slacks and socks—

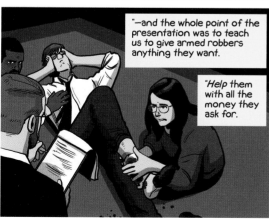
"—and the whole point of the presentation was to teach us to give armed robbers anything they want.

"*Help* them with all the money they ask for.

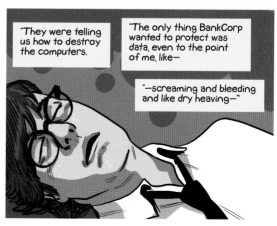
"They were telling us how to destroy the computers.

"The only thing BankCorp wanted to protect was data, even to the point of me, like—

"—screaming and bleeding and like dry heaving—"

Wow.
So you weren't really shot.
Shot at, maybe.
I was so.
You maybe hurt yourself on a bullet but—
How dare you.
—whoop—

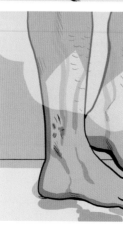

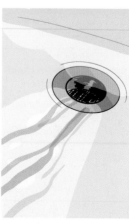

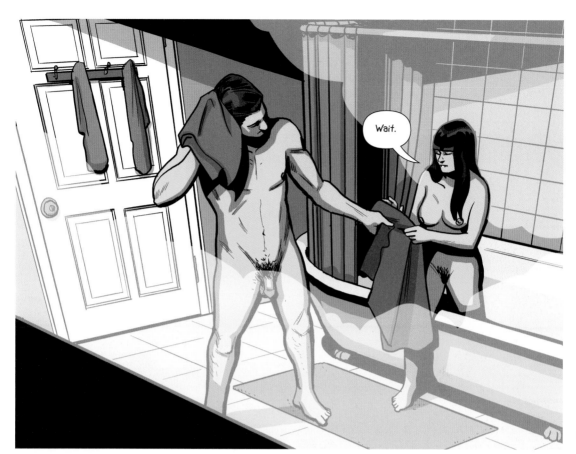

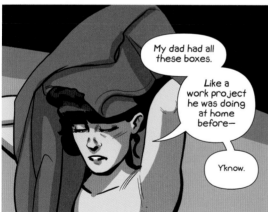

My dad had all these boxes.

Like a work project he was doing at home before—

Yknow.

"When I was living with my mom before—

"Yknow.

"I looked at it.

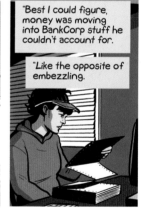

"Best I could figure, money was moving into BankCorp stuff he couldn't account for.

"Like the opposite of embezzling.

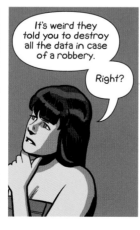

"There were more and more of these ghost deposits. Never a ton, but enough to be enough.

"I didn't get all the way through."

It's weird they told you to destroy all the data in case of a robbery.

Right?

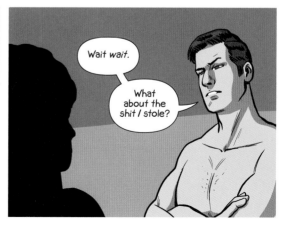

Wait wait.

What about the shit I stole?

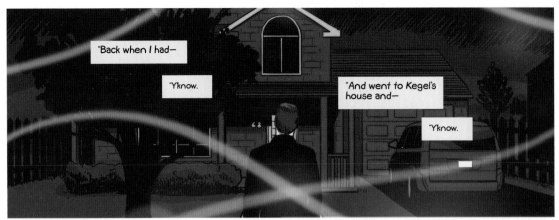

"Back when I had—

"Yknow.

"And went to Kegel's house and—

"Yknow.

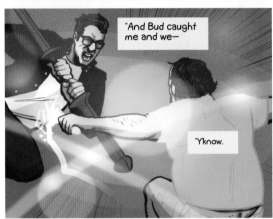

"And Bud caught me and we—

"Yknow.

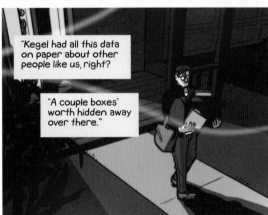

"Kegel had all this data on paper about other people like us, right?

"A couple boxes' worth hidden away over there."

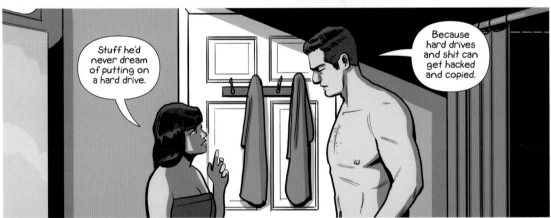

Stuff he'd never dream of putting on a hard drive.

Because hard drives and shit can get hacked and copied.

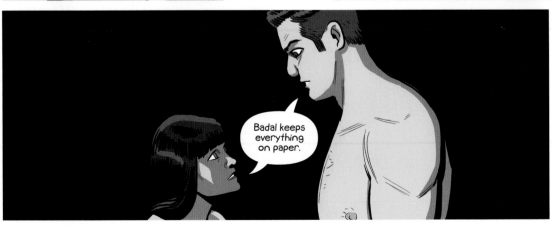

Badal keeps everything on paper.

Did we figure something out?
It feels like we figured something out.
I mean— I guess?
Maybe?
Whatever he's up to—
—whatever his whole goal is, tracking people like us or whatever—
He keeps on paper.
Destroyable, steal-abAAHH—
stop
before it's too late, Kuber.
You see, I've been waiting my whole life for this.
—UZE?!
Suze, honey—?!
AAhhhokay I'm okay—
What the hell was that? Did it happen again?
Yeah—
Yeah, I just—
AMERICA
—I think I need to go see a doctor.

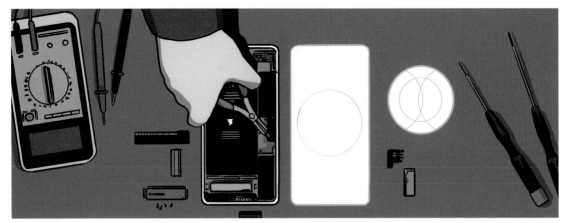

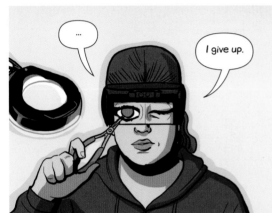

...

I give up.

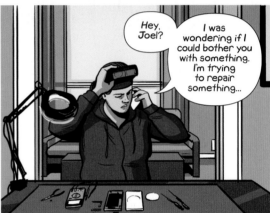

Hey, Joel?

I was wondering if I could bother you with something. I'm trying to repair something...

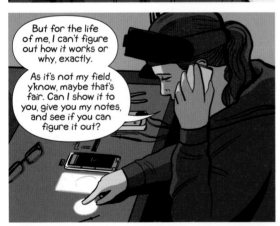

But for the life of me, I can't figure out how it works or why, exactly.

As it's not my field, y'know, maybe that's fair. Can I show it to you, give you my notes, and see if you can figure it out?

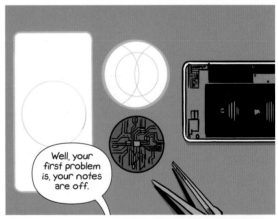

Well, your first problem is, your notes are off.

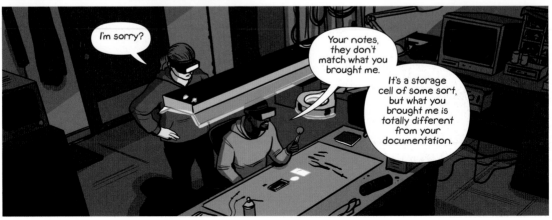

I'm sorry?

Your notes, they don't match what you brought me.

It's a storage cell of some sort, but what you brought me is totally different from your documentation.

...
The fuck you say?
Here, look—
So here's what you drew— it's like a little PV panel from a solar battery almost. Which is weird because it's hidden, but okay.
I *think* that's what this looks like, anyway. But look at the actual thing, Dr. Kincaid...
The array— the layout—they're entirely different. I don't know why or what it even does yet, but this doesn't match the drawing.
Maybe you lost a piece or misplaced it—
—no no no...
... I don't understand. I was extra—
—extra—
—fastidious with my notes, especially because I felt so over my head.
Unless...
Dr. Kincaid...?
Are you all right?
Yeah, I just moved my head too fast and everything's so magnified it made me feel like I was gonna throw up.

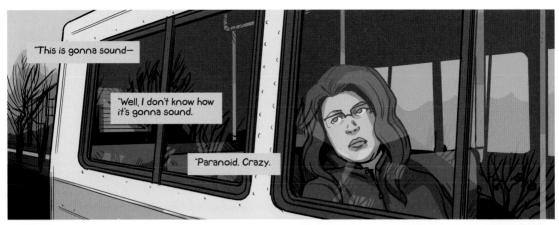

"This is gonna sound—

"Well, I don't know how it's gonna sound.

"Paranoid. Crazy.

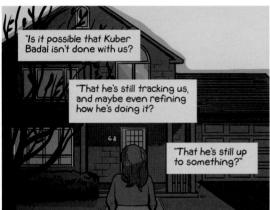

"Is it possible that Kuber Badal isn't done with us?

"That he's still tracking us, and maybe even refining how he's doing it?

"That he's still up to something?"

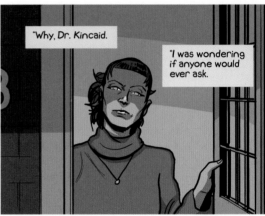

"Why, Dr. Kincaid.

"I was wondering if anyone would ever ask.

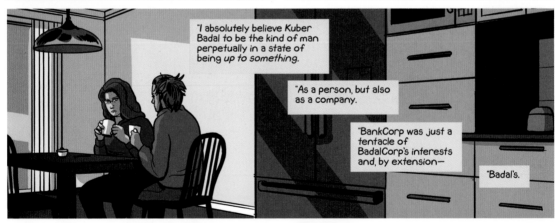

"I absolutely believe Kuber Badal to be the kind of man perpetually in a state of being *up to something.*

"As a person, but also as a company.

"BankCorp was just a tentacle of BadalCorp's interests and, by extension—

"Badal's.

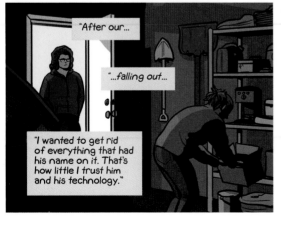

"After our...

"...falling out...

"I wanted to get rid of everything that had his name on it. That's how little I trust him and his technology."

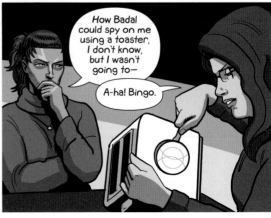

How Badal could spy on me using a toaster, I don't know, but I wasn't going to—

A-ha! Bingo.

Everything he manufactures has these in them.
They're like little solar cells that make calculators run. Only instead of sunlight...
"... we power them. However we all do what we do, it produces a discharge of energy.
"These capture them. Like little traps getting filled, and they radio home."
Oh my god.
His big battery.
I have no idea what you're talking about.
I always assumed it was a metaphor or, or, or—
—he has a secret room. Off of his office.
We were never allowed inside. He'd just say—
—charging my batteries, Mrs. Spurge.
Be right back.
I found one of those discs and tried to determine what it was.
Then suddenly the disc didn't match my drawing.
I wondered if Badal swapped it out.
Could he actually have a battery? Do people like us—
We need to—
—I'll drive.

We have reason to believe that whatever Kuber Badal is up to, we—
People like us, with our abilities—
—remain of key importance to him.
I'm sorry?
We aren't sure what exactly, or why or how, but he's keeping track of all of us still.
And he's refining how he tracks us.
I think he upgraded a component inside of a BadalCorp device in my possession personally.
It was a collection cell like on a solar-powered calculator.
Only it's not solar energy he collects from us.
He has a battery of his own design inside his office. A secret project.
What if we're powering it somehow?
I don't understand.
To what end?
You said it yourself.
Badal fucks people.
I meant he's dangerous. I meant we shouldn't fuck back.
Right, but what if...
Unknowingly, unwittingly, and unwillingly...
...we've been the ones who make it all possible?

Ooh!
PLEASE HOLD STILL MA'AM.
Aaah—!
Um, hello?
I'm sorry to ask, but, how much longer?
THIS IS YOUR BRAIN ON DRUGS.
AH, SHIT. WE BETTER INVENT THE MRI MACHINE
MA'AM.
sorryowOWOW—
ZZZK
That was my fault. I'm sorry.
Sorry sorry sorry—
Wrrrrrrrrr

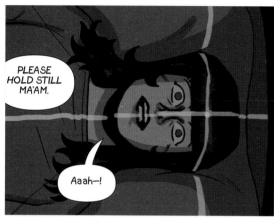

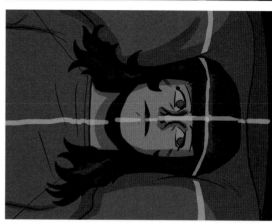

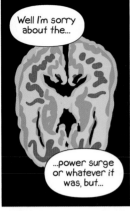

Well I'm sorry about the...

...power surge or whatever it was, but...

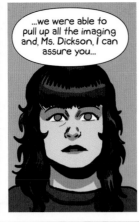

...we were able to pull up all the imaging and, Ms. Dickson, I can assure you...

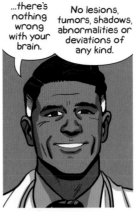

...there's nothing wrong with your brain.

No lesions, tumors, shadows, abnormalities or deviations of any kind.

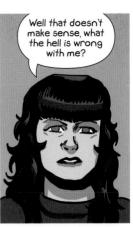

Well that doesn't make sense, what the hell is wrong with me?

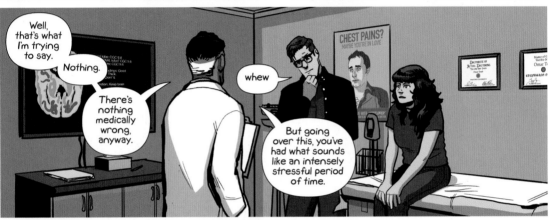

Well, that's what I'm trying to say.

Nothing.

There's nothing medically wrong, anyway.

whew

But going over this, you've had what sounds like an intensely stressful period of time.

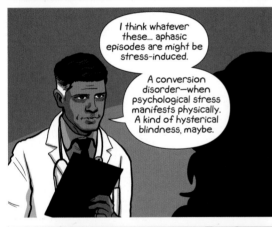

I think whatever these... aphasic episodes are might be stress-induced.

A conversion disorder—when psychological stress manifests physically. A kind of hysterical blindness, maybe.

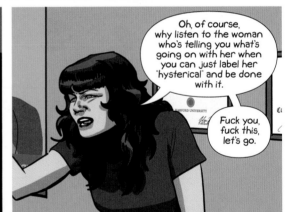

Oh, of course, why listen to the woman who's telling you what's going on with her when you can just label her "hysterical" and be done with it.

Fuck you, fuck this, let's go.

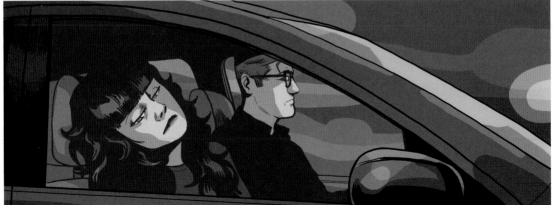

sigh

let's go.

Security Sound!
Security Sound!
Security Sound!
Securi-
—yes yes, all right.
Oh my.
What an unexpected surprise.
Badal.

It took me a long time to admit that I knew you'd lied to me.
And it took even longer to admit that I was okay with it. That I was okay with us playing sex-cop make-believe.
Because it meant power. Order. Control.
And I wanted it. I got off on it.
That's on me, and that's why I'm here.
I don't know how to fix what I did, but I think I know how to fix what's happened because of it.
All the people we chased, hunted down, spied on, intimidated—
You're going to leave them alone.
I ever get word, ever again, that you're so much as a shadow of you, in any of their lives—
I'm going to shoot you in the fucking head.
Ask yourself if I'm playing make-believe now, asshole.
Oh my.
I'm sorry you had to hear all that...

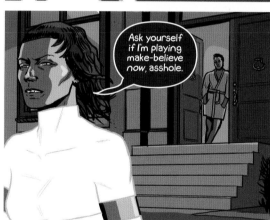

... I thought she would never leave.
Don't you find guests like that to be a bore?
Forgive my rudeness. I know what you want, and I know why you're here, but I hope you'll do me the pleasure of saying it anyway.
You see, I've been waiting my whole life for this.
I want to talk to you ... about the future.

PASSIN' haha ha ha LAFFS!
with BUD & DEWEY ha ha
A man goes to his doctor because he's depressed.
He says, "Doctor, help me! I'm depressed!
"Food has no taste anymore, I hate my job, I never see anyone and I never talk to anybody.
"I wake up in the middle of the night because I've been crying in my sleep, and then I realize how *sad* that is and I just cry more!
"Doc, I really think I'm gonna end it all!"
Well the doctor, he isn't worried.
He claps his hands together and laughs!
"This one's easy!," the doctor says to Pagliacci, "And all you—"
Son of a *bitch*—
Wait, what happened to the guy?
Was he okay?
More laffs next time!!!

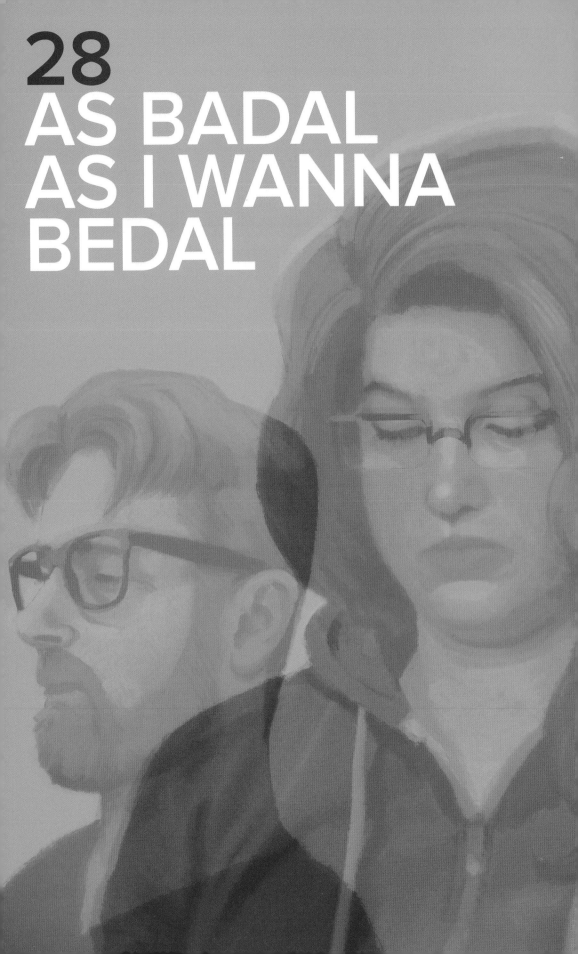

28
AS BADAL
AS I WANNA
BEDAL

I'd offer you a drink, but this is very expensive.
Not that you're not worth it, but we both know you don't have a drink tonight.
And we both know that because...
...we've already seen it before.
Haven't we?
Yeah.
Yeah, we have.
Well then. Since we both know what happens next...
Let's get to *what happens next*, shall we?
Come on.

Where are we going?
Ha.
Wow.
Seriously?
The *road*, watch the road—
All right, all right...
...I'll say it if you want me to say it.
We're going to where it all *started*.
BADADDY

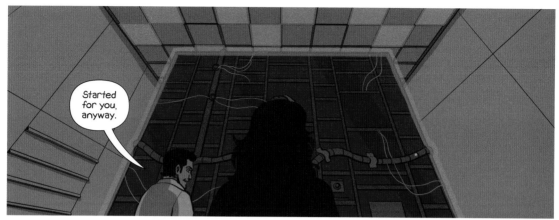

Started for you, anyway.

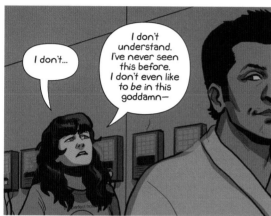

I don't...

I don't understand. I've never seen this before. I don't even like to *be* in this goddamn—

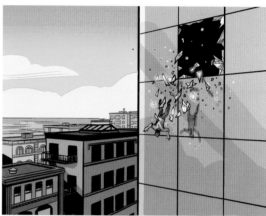

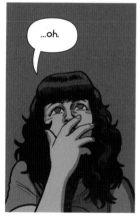

...oh.

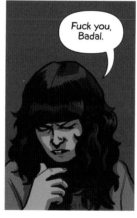

Fuck you, Badal.

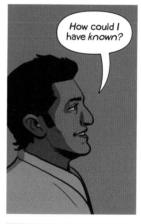

How could I have *known*?

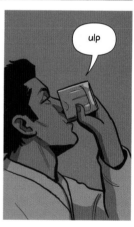

ulp

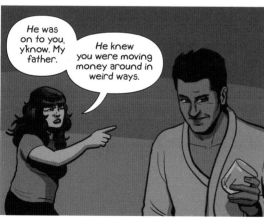

He was on to you, yknow. My father.

He knew you were moving money around in weird ways.

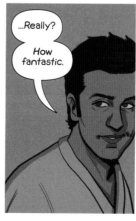

...Really?

How fantastic.

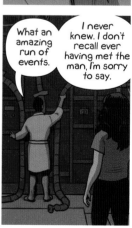

What an amazing run of events.

I never knew. I don't recall ever having met the man, I'm sorry to say.

But look how he's brought us all together.
The money I made in the micro-crash before your father's death allowed me to finally build *A.N.T.O.N.I.O.*
What's it do?
It's...
It's like a battery, you could say.
Who was he?
Oh come on, you *know.*
Bah, *fine,* okay, you want to play your games, play your games.
But I've been waiting a long time for tonight, and I'd appreciate simply getting down to it.
No no no, hang the fuck on—
—I don't know who you think I am or what you think I'm here for, but I guarantee you, it's not that.
Pff. Please, you're about one foot and *nine girthy inches* from being anything remotely resembling my type.
And I know exactly who you are.
You're *God.*

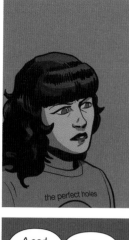

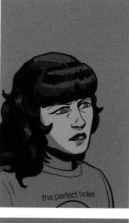

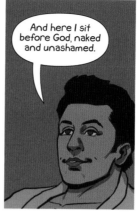
And here I sit before God, naked and unashamed.

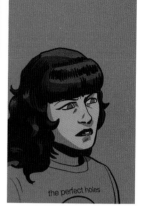

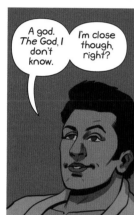
A god. *The* God, I don't know.

I'm close though, right?

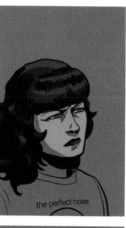

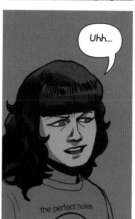
Uhh...

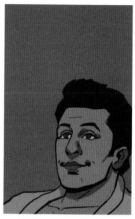

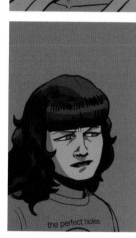

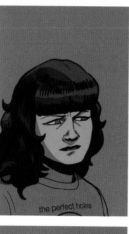

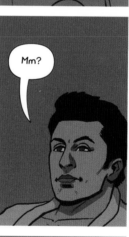
Mm?

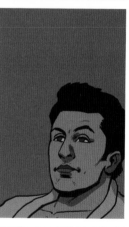

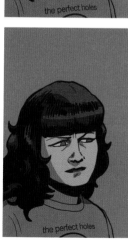

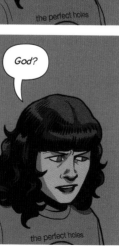
God?

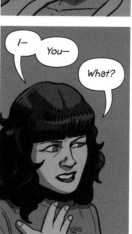
I—

You—

What?

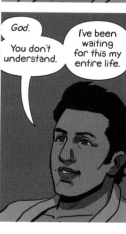
God. You don't understand.

I've been waiting for this my entire life.

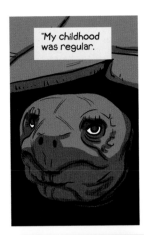

"My childhood was regular.

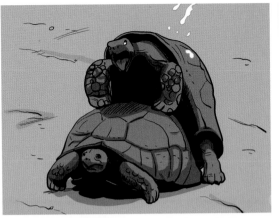

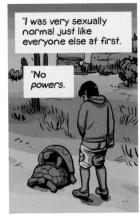

"I was very sexually normal just like everyone else at first.

"No powers.

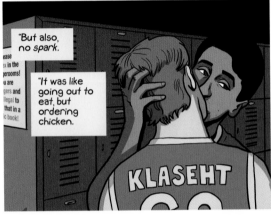

"But also, no *spark*.

"It was like going out to eat, but ordering chicken.

KLASEHT

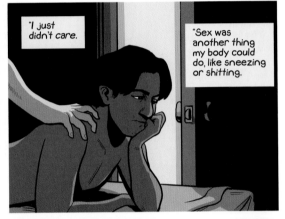

"I just didn't *care*.

"Sex was another thing my body could do, like sneezing or shitting.

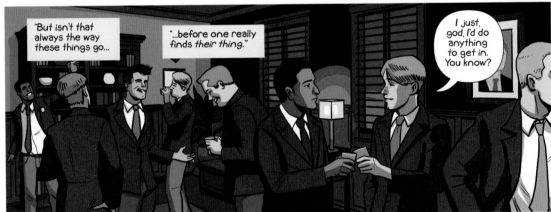

"But isn't that always the way these things go...

"...before one really finds *their thing*."

I just, god, I'd do anything to get in. You know?

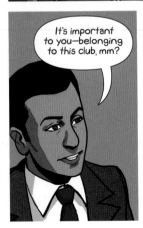

It's important to you—belonging to this club, mm?

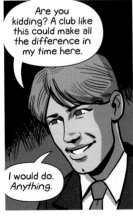

Are you kidding? A club like this could make all the difference in my time here.

I would do. *Anything*.

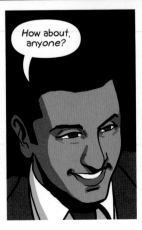

How about, anyone?

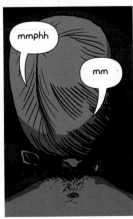

mmphh

mm

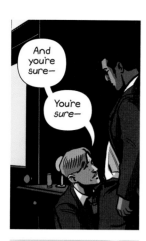

And you're sure—

You're sure—

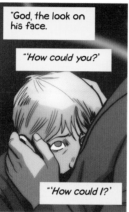

JESUS, I didn't say STOP don't—

Aah—

—You—

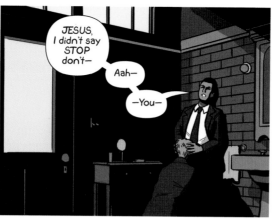

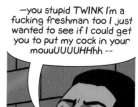

—you stupid TWINK I'm a fucking freshman too I just wanted to see if I could get you to put my cock in your mouuUUUUHHhh --

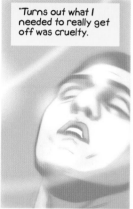

"Turns out what I needed to really get off was cruelty."

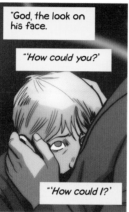

"God, the look on his face.

"'How could you?'

"'How could I?'"

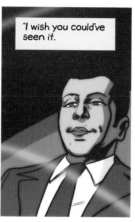

"I wish you could've seen it."

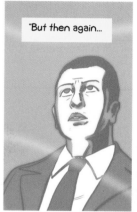

"But then again..."

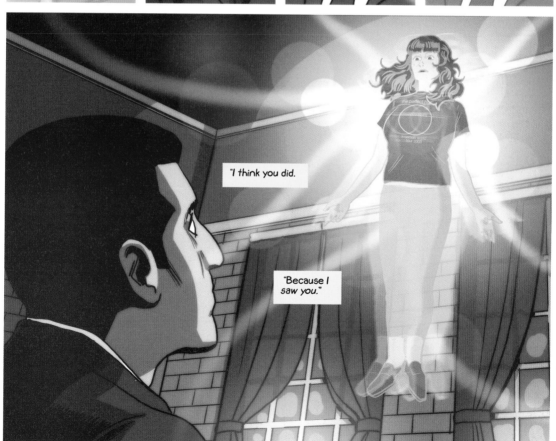

"I think you did.

"Because I saw you."

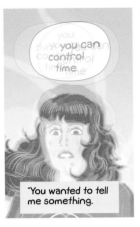
"you can control time"

"You wanted to tell me something.

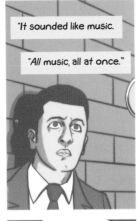
"It sounded like music.

"All music, all at once."

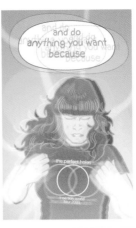
"and do anything you want because"

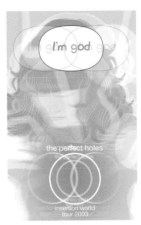
"I'm god"

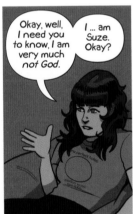
"But I'd heard enough."

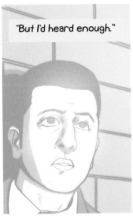
I would set about life with renewed purpose and do what you had commanded.

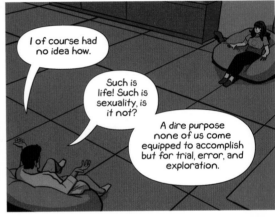
I of course had no idea how.

Such is life! Such is sexuality, is it not?

A dire purpose none of us come equipped to accomplish but for trial, error, and exploration.

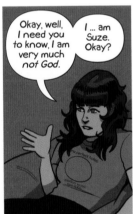
Okay, well, I need you to know, I am very much *not* God.

I ... am Suze. Okay?

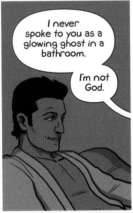
I never spoke to you as a glowing ghost in a bathroom.

I'm not God.

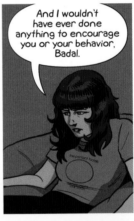
And I wouldn't have ever done anything to encourage you or your behavior, Badal.

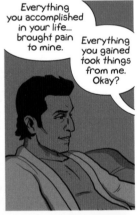
Everything you accomplished in your life... brought pain to mine.

Everything you gained took things from me. Okay?

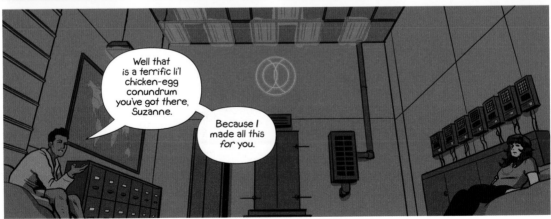
Well that is a terrific li'l chicken-egg conundrum you've got there, Suzanne.

Because I made all this for you.

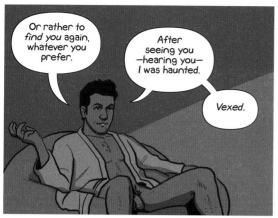

Or rather to *find you* again, whatever you prefer.

After seeing you —hearing you— I was haunted.

Vexed.

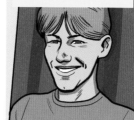

"Antonio stuck around for two years after that, bless his heart.

"And the sex was never anything more than just that: sex.

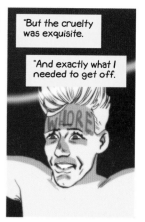

"But the cruelty was exquisite.

"And exactly what I needed to get off.

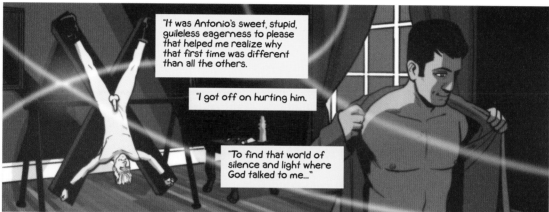

"It was Antonio's sweet, stupid, guileless eagerness to please that helped me realize why that first time was different than all the others.

"I got off on hurting him.

"To find that world of silence and light where God talked to me..."

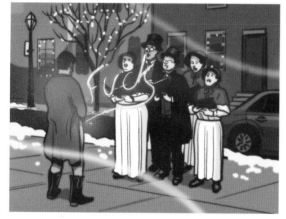

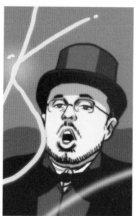

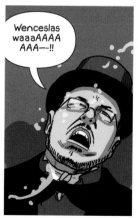

Wenceslas waaaAAAAAAA—!!

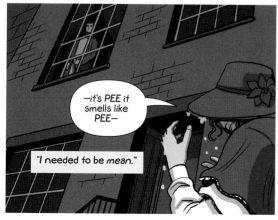

—it's PEE it smells like PEE—

"I needed to be *mean*."

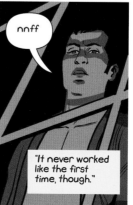

nnff

"It never worked like the first time, though."

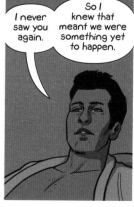

I never saw you again.

So I knew that meant we were something yet to happen.

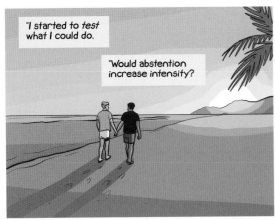

"I started to *test* what I could do.

"Would abstention increase intensity?

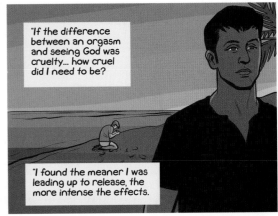

"If the difference between an orgasm and seeing God was cruelty... how cruel did I need to be?

"I found the meaner I was leading up to release, the more intense the effects.

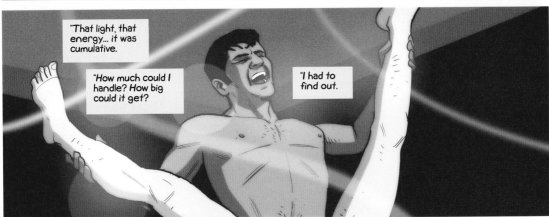

"That light, that energy... it was cumulative.

"How much could I handle? How big could it get?

"I had to find out.

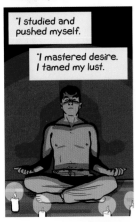

"I studied and pushed myself.

"I mastered desire. I tamed my lust.

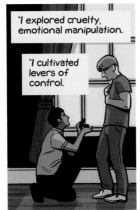

"I explored cruelty, emotional manipulation.

"I cultivated levers of control.

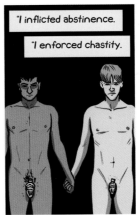

"I inflicted abstinence.

"I enforced chastity.

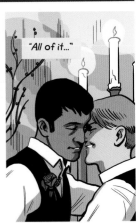

"All of it..."

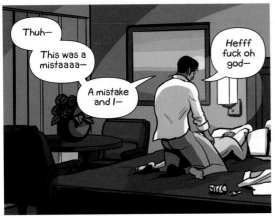

Thuh—

This was a mistaaaa—

A mistake and I—

Hefff fuck oh god—

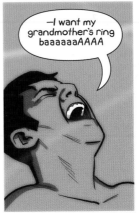

—I want my grandmother's ring baaaaaaAAAA

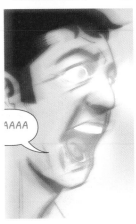

AAAA

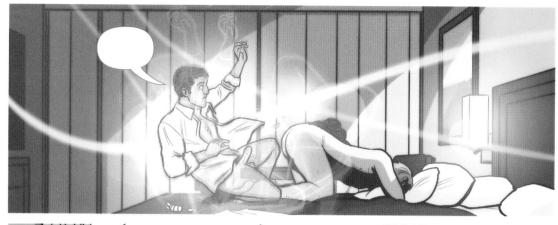

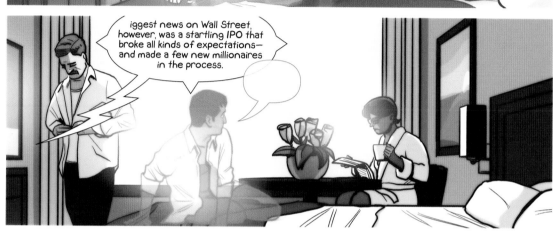

iggest news on Wall Street, however, was a startling IPO that broke all kinds of expectations—and made a few new millionaires in the process.

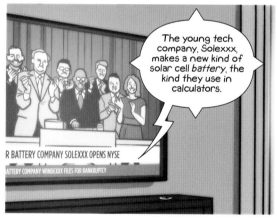

The young tech company, Solexxx, makes a new kind of solar cell *battery*, the kind they use in calculators.

R BATTERY COMPANY SOLEXXX OPENS NYSE
ATTERY COMPANY WINDEXXX FILES FOR BANKRUPTCY

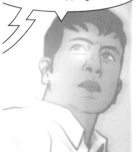

Its stock started the day valued at a modest three dollars a share, and by the time the bell rang, it closed at a jaw-dropping 446—

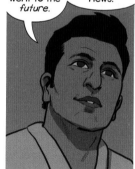

I came so hard I went to the *future*.

Lucky for me, the future was watching the news.

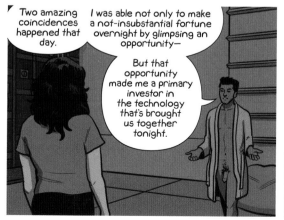

Two amazing coincidences happened that day.

I was able not only to make a not-insubstantial fortune overnight by glimpsing an opportunity—

But that opportunity made me a primary investor in the technology that's brought us together tonight.

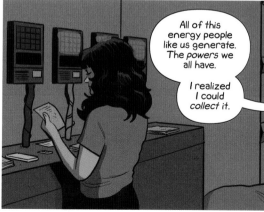

All of this energy people like us generate. The *powers* we all have.

I realized I could *collect* it.

You can tell me now—
How do we go backwards? How much energy must I gather, how much will it take?
Do you and I need to experience orgasm at the same *time* or—
You *can't* go backwards, Badal.
That's the whole thing.
I'm sorry that I'm not who you think I am.
I'm just *me*.
Yes, Suzanne.
You. You're the only o
ne that ma
AAAFUCK—!
Fuck fuck FUCK—
—not AGAIN—

BADAL I SWEAR TO YOU
tters.
Are you all right?
AAhh—
—shit—
What the fucking FUCK is fucking WRONG WITH ME?!?
What? I—
You? Nothing.
Don't you see?
It's getting closer now.
Our apotheosis.
And I really wish you'd put your dick away.
I get that a lot.
So? Let's get on with it.
I don't know...
WHAT THE FUCK YOU'RE TALKING ABOUT!

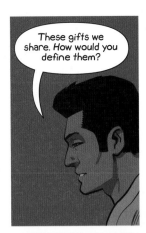

These gifts we share. *How* would you define them?

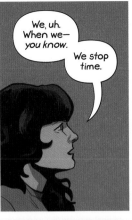

We, uh. When we— *you know.*

We stop time.

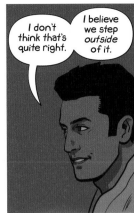

I don't think that's quite right.

I believe we step *outside* of it.

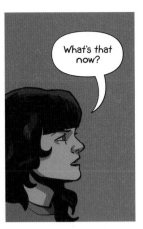

What's that now?

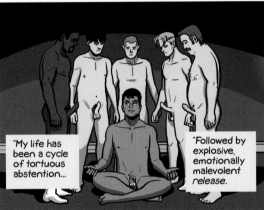

"My life has been a cycle of tortuous abstention...

"Followed by explosive, emotionally malevolent release.

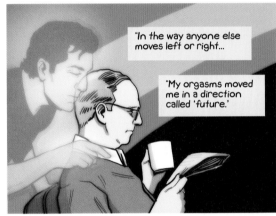

"In the way anyone else moves left or right...

"My orgasms moved me in a direction called 'future.'

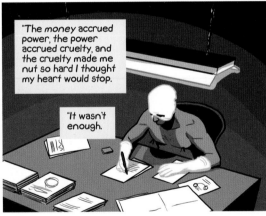

"The *money* accrued power, the power accrued cruelty, and the cruelty made me nut so hard I thought my heart would stop.

"It wasn't enough.

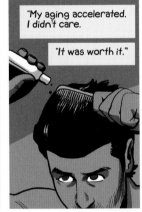

"My aging accelerated. I didn't care.

"It was worth it."

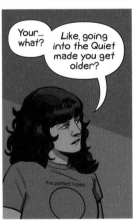

Your... what?

Like, going into the Quiet made you get older?

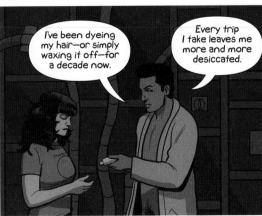

I've been dyeing my hair—or simply waxing it off—for a decade now.

Every trip I take leaves me more and more desiccated.

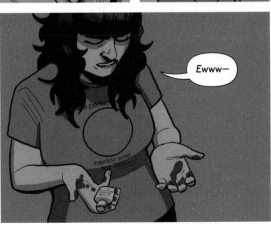

Ewww—

The point, my dear Suzanne, is this: up has its down. Left has its right.
So must *future* have its *past*.
I built A.N.T.O.N.I.O., all the BadalCorp technology, the Sex Police— everything—
To trap enough energy to go "past" just as I'm capable of going "future."
You...
MMMMmmm?
So you'd have an orgasm... and all the energy you trapped...
You could go back.
And if I go forward and inform my path...
...
You could...
Go back and...
Oh god.
You think you can change the past.

Fuck yes I do!
I called it our apotheosis because that is exactly what tonight is: the crescendo of our lives to date—
—the moment to which every *other* moment has built: our *now*.
I listened to what you told me all those years ago.
And *everything* I've done was to make *now* happen.
My life, my work, my fortune, all of it has gone to this.
Our exalted elevation!
insertion world tour 2003
"*Spurge* needed to feel like she was a force for *law* and *order*.
"I convinced *her* we were protecting our kind.
"Bud wanted to feel power and control...
"...and he was so self-hating he gave me the power and control to abuse him.
"The companies and corporations were all opportunity and will given shape and form.
ADALCOR
"They all made traps."
All so we could *fuck time* as much as time has *fucked us*.
All so we could stop life and rewrite it however we see fit!

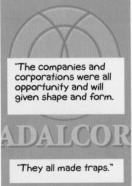

That's why I did it all, Suzanne.
What do you want? Name it. You want your father?
Let's bring him back.
Jesus, what now?
I don't think it's supposed to work that way.
Life doesn't stop, ever.
We can't go back, only forward.
BUT THIS IS WHAT YOU TOLD ME TO DO, YOU STUPID BITCH!
Heff
Heff
Fuck you look hot when you cry.
nnn.
fwump

God, the look on your face.
What?
You should be happy.
Stop! Please!
Ha.
Couldn't even if I wanted toooo—
oooOHHHH A.N.T.O.N.I.O. no teeth no TEETH—
fwump

AAAFUCK—!
stop
Fuck fuck FUCK—
—not AGAIN—
before it's too late, Kuber.
There's still
time
BADAL I SWEAR TO YOU
You think you can control time and do anything that you want because I'm God—
—but you're wr

BADALC

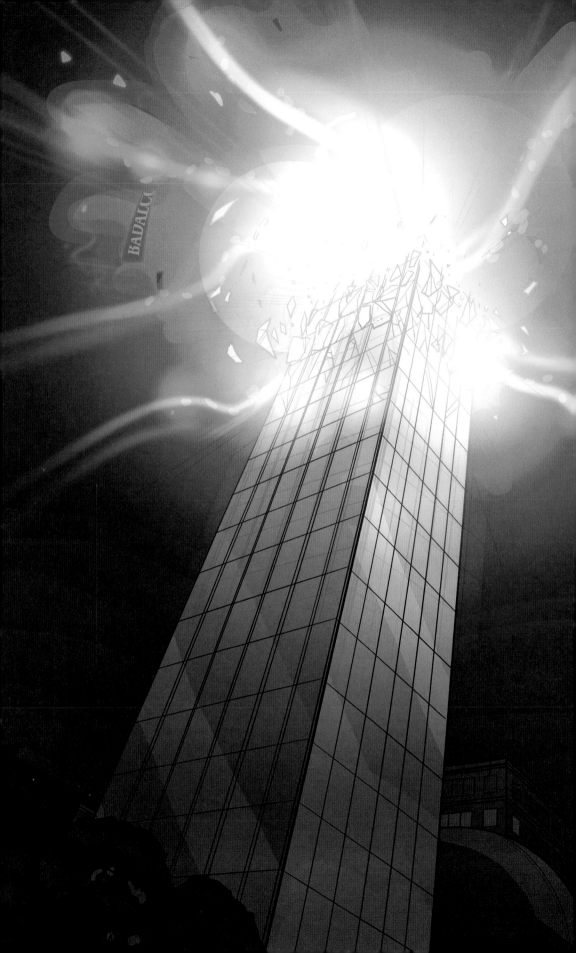

PASSIN' haha ha ha LAFFS!
with BUD & DEWEY ha ha
So there's this family act, right? A whole family of little entertainers. And they go to see a talent agent, hoping for representation.
And the agent says, "Oh, great! I love family acts. They're so wholesome and delightful!"
He sits back, puts his feet up, and says "Show me what you got!"
And the family they start their act but it's—like, it's gross.
It's... it's super, super gross.
What is?
The act.
What do you mean by "gross"?
What kind of stuff do they do?
Well, like...
Good lord.
What would you even call that act?
WHY WOULD THEY DO THAT? WHY WOULD THEY CALL IT THAT?!?
THAT IS A TERRIBLE NAME FOR A TERRIBLE ACT!
No, Dewey, honey, wait—
More laffs next time!!!

29
O.D.D.

SIX DAYS LATER:
Shit, no, no wait.
It didn't happen like this.
Well, I mean, it *did*, but not in this order. Hang on—

THE NEXT DAY, FOR REAL THIS TIME:

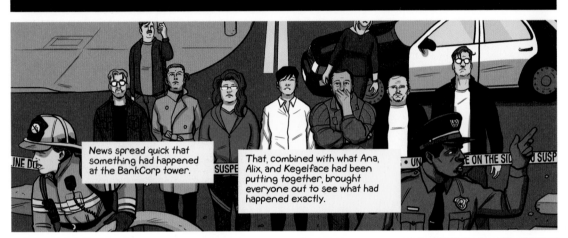

News spread quick that something had happened at the BankCorp tower.

That, combined with what Ana, Alix, and Kegelface had been putting together, brought everyone out to see what had happened exactly.

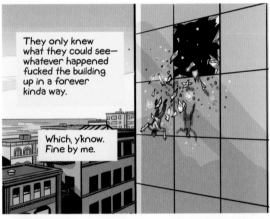

They only knew what they could see—whatever happened fucked the building up in a forever kinda way.

Which, yknow. Fine by me.

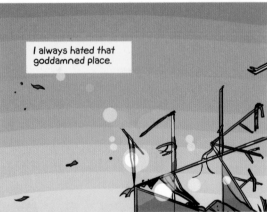

I always hated that goddamned place.

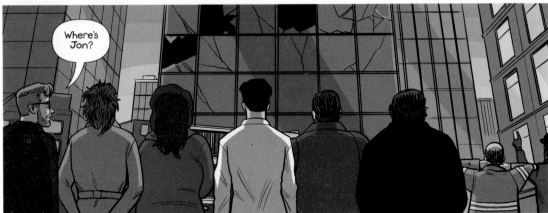

Where's Jon?

It was a good question.

After the explosion—

—nobody could ever figure out what else to call it—

—Badal and I both went missing.

And, after seeing what had happened to Badal's suite...

...Jon knew that, whatever happened, it had happened to us both.

So for a minute there, he was gone too.

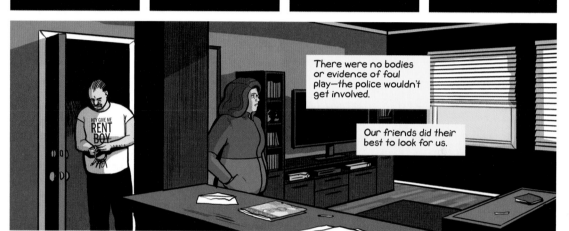

There were no bodies or evidence of foul play—the police wouldn't get involved.

Our friends did their best to look for us.

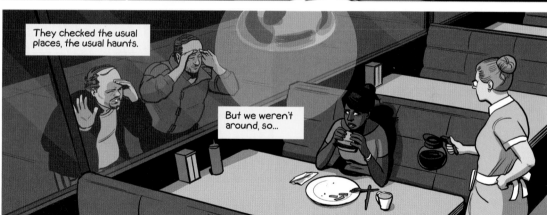

They checked the usual places, the usual haunts.

But we weren't around, so...

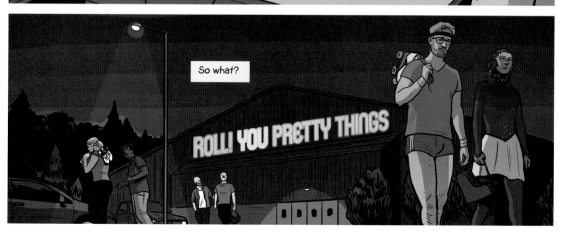

So what?

ROLL! YOU PRETTY THINGS

After a while, what could they do?
What could anybody do?
Sometimes people just disappear.
And sometimes they take pieces of us with them when they go.
TROBOY
nnnf–
heff
heff
Shoot.
Sh–
SHOOT!
TROBOY
Bud!
Bud, something's wrong–
Dewey and Bud figured it out first.
Kegel was next.
Holy shit, Mrs. Spurge?!?

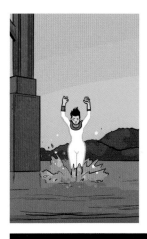
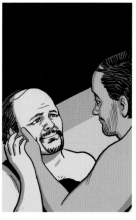
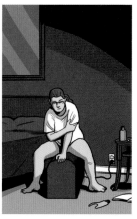
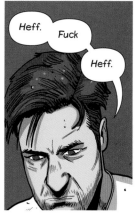

The Quiet
was gone.

For everyone.

Jon wouldn't
figure it out
for a while.

He was
getting busy.

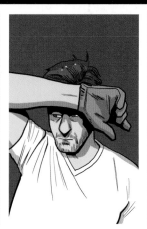
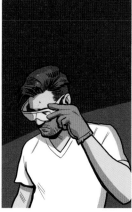

Well, a
different
kind of busy.

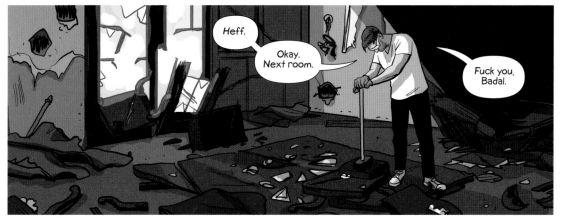

The police would find him
26 hours after he left the scene
of the accident.

In Kuber Badal's mansion.

Where he'd been that entire time.

Getting busy.

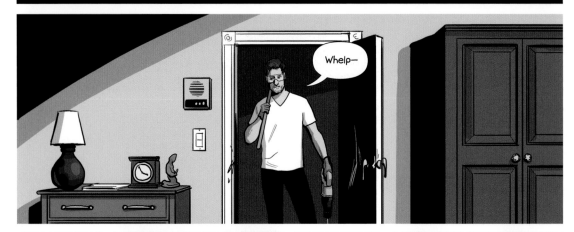

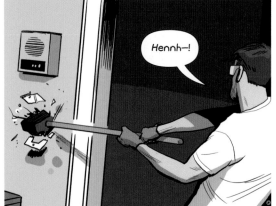

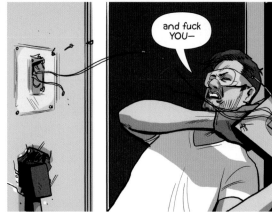

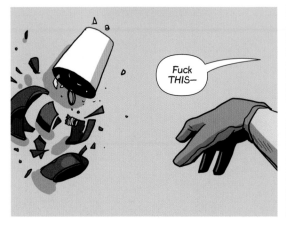

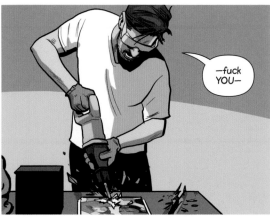

rrah
and—
He'd decided he was going to destroy everything he found inside.
Fuck all of these guys—
Everything.
Fuck—
Because, it's Jon, of course he meant it literally.
—YOU—
—and—
—YOU—
—and YOU—
—and—
Can you imagine?
This fucking guy.

Huhhh.
Shit.
And fuck every part of this goddamn—
Ahhh, shit.

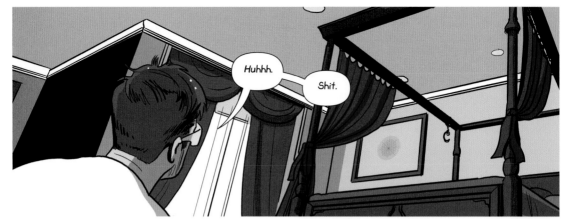

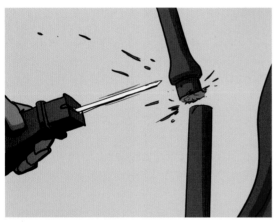

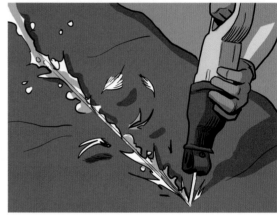

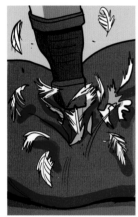

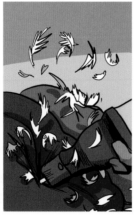

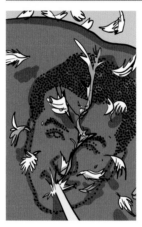

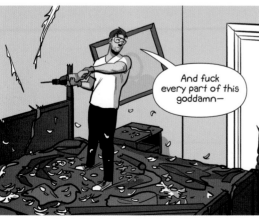

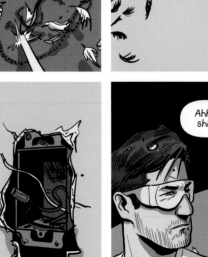

Whoa–
Heh.
Shit.
Okay.
C'mon.

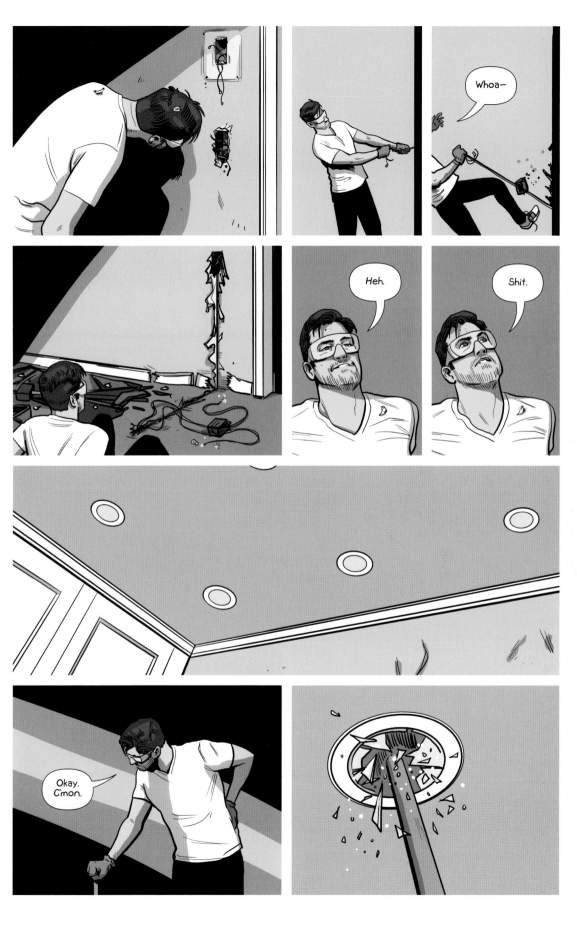

shit
SHIT—
It wasn't an exact science.
I mean, think about it.
How much *stuff* is there, in all your stuff.
How much work you'd have to do to render it all entirely useless.

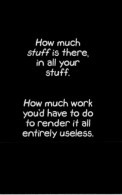

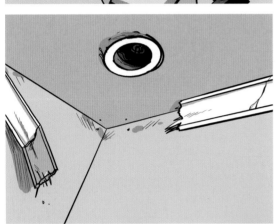

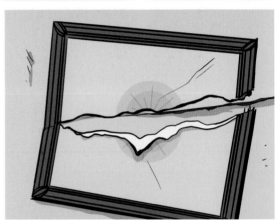

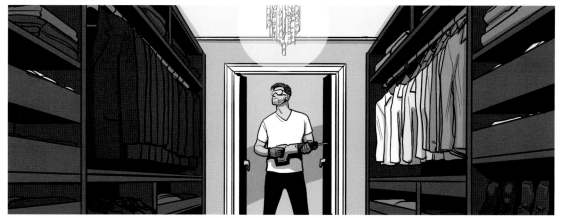

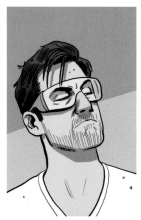

Later on, he'd call it obsessive-destructive disorder.

I thought he was kidding.

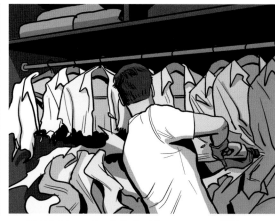

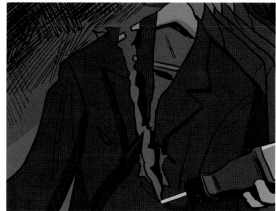

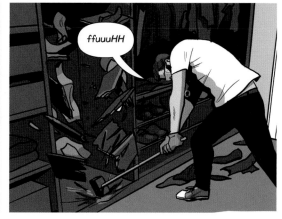

ffuuuHH

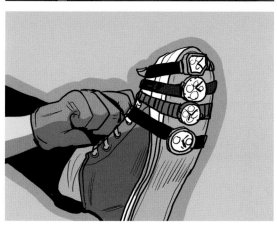

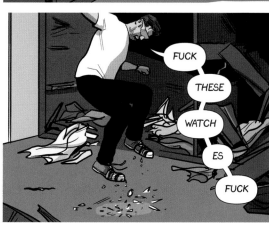

FUCK
THESE
WATCH
ES
FUCK

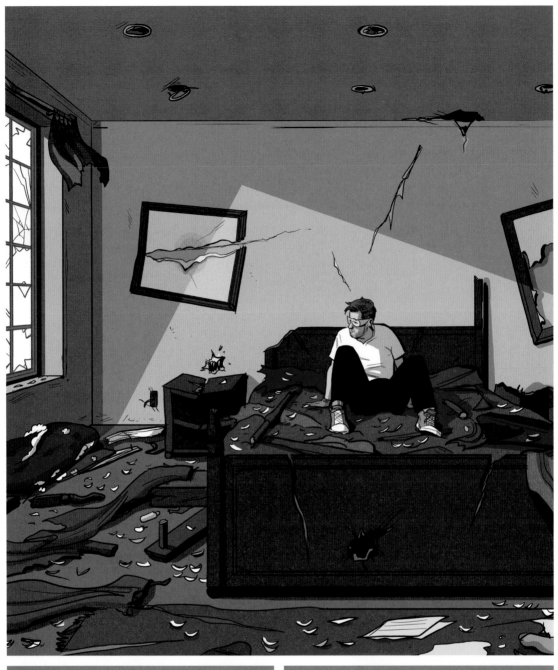

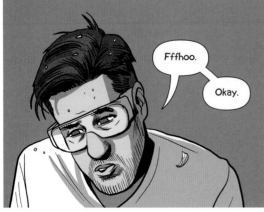

Fffhoo.

Okay.

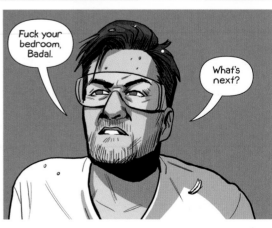

Fuck your bedroom, Badal.

What's next?

nnnah—

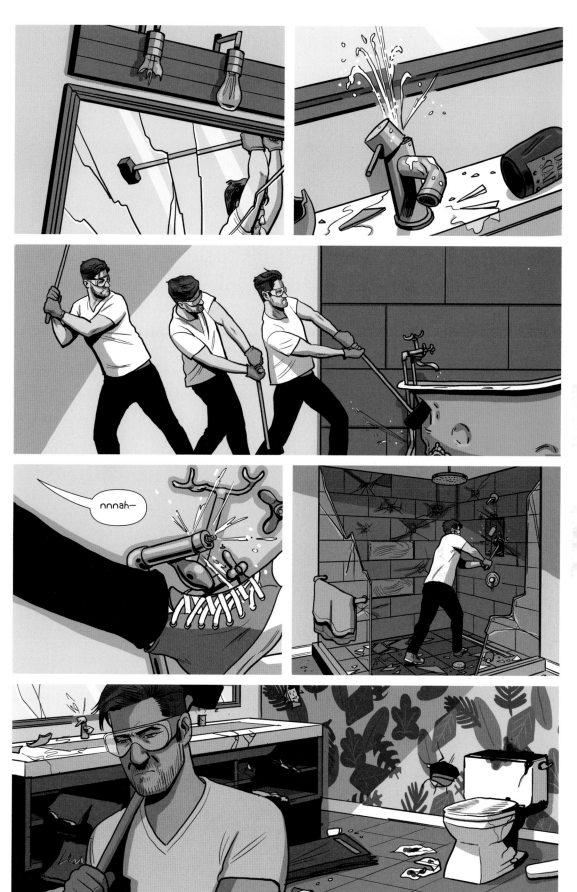

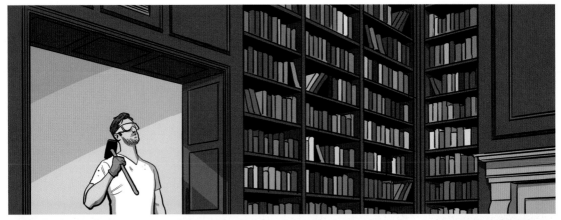

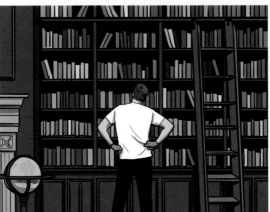

The library presented him with a problem.

He didn't want to destroy the books.

For me.

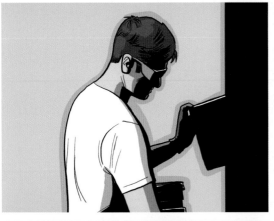

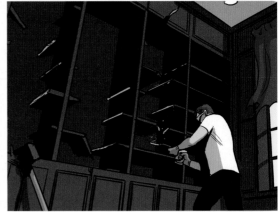

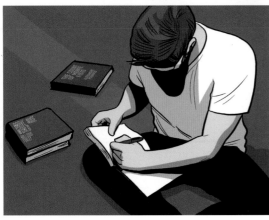

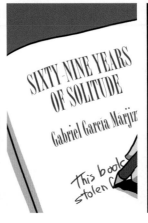

SIXTY-NINE YEARS OF SOLITUDE

Gabriel García Márjiz

This book stolen f

He wrote, "This book stolen from a real asshole named Kuber Badal."

In every
single book.

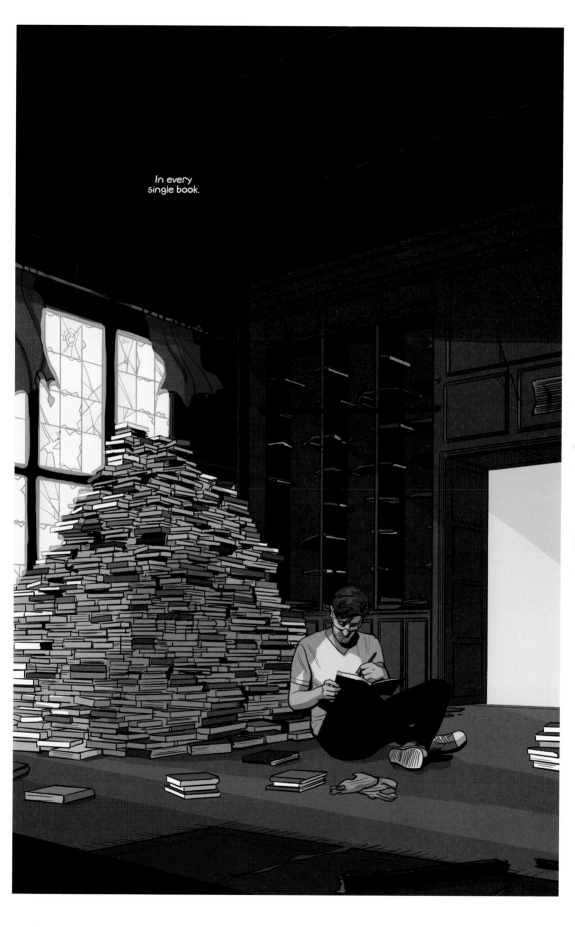

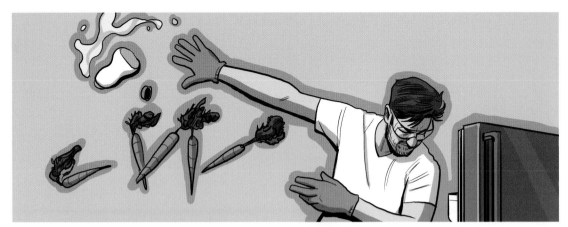

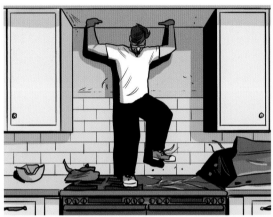

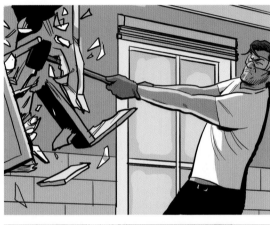

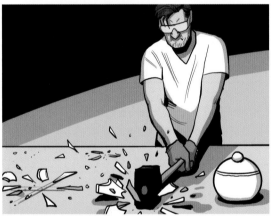

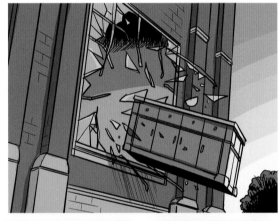

Even the
flatware.

Ow.

Goddammit.

Even the
tines on
every fork.

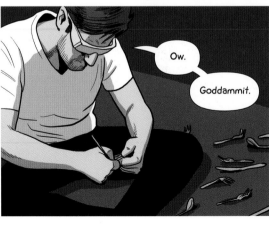

And I know this was, at its core, an explosion of his grief and, quite frankly, mental illness.

I mean, obsessive-destructive disorder was exactly right.

So I don't mean to make light.

But at some point it occurred to me—

—I don't know why—

—and, again, sorry—

—that this kind of intensity and obsession over details that could just explode out of him—

—is what made him good in bed.

I mean, find someone who'll fuck up individual oyster forks for you, and you'll have someone who makes sure your shit's taken care of. Yknow?

But then I felt awful for thinking it.

Because, I mean, look at him.

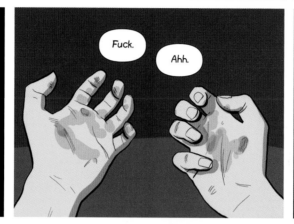

Fuck.

Ahh.

He's in so much pain.

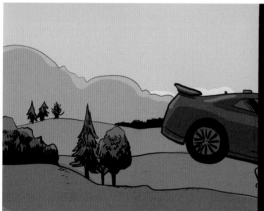

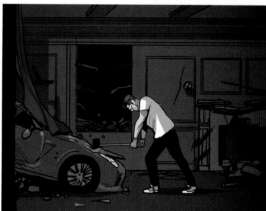

And he feels so much of it, and it feels so huge, the only way he can deal with it is to get it outside of his body.

Any way he can.

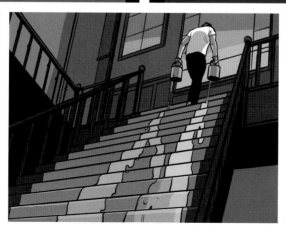

He told me once he feels like he doesn't have skin in all the same places normal people do.

Good things, bad things—

—he feels them all *too much*.

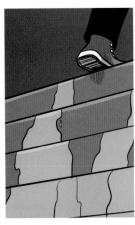

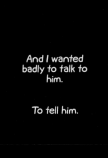

And I wanted badly to talk to him.

To tell him.

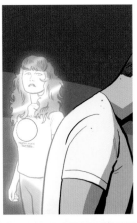

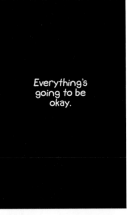

Everything's going to be okay.

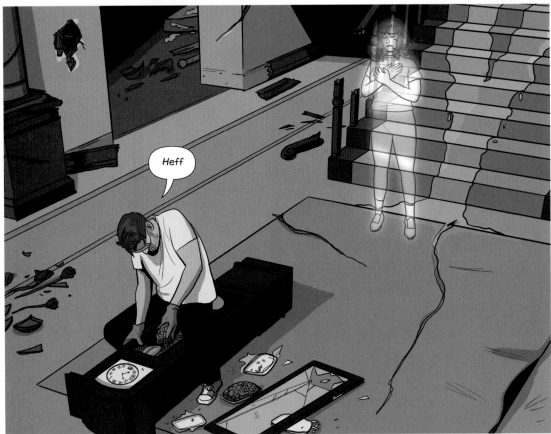

Heff

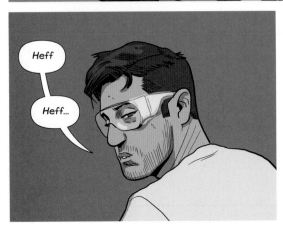

Heff

Heff...

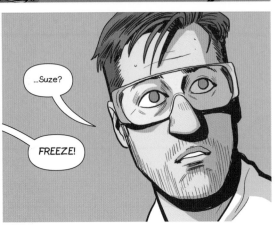

...Suze?

FREEZE!

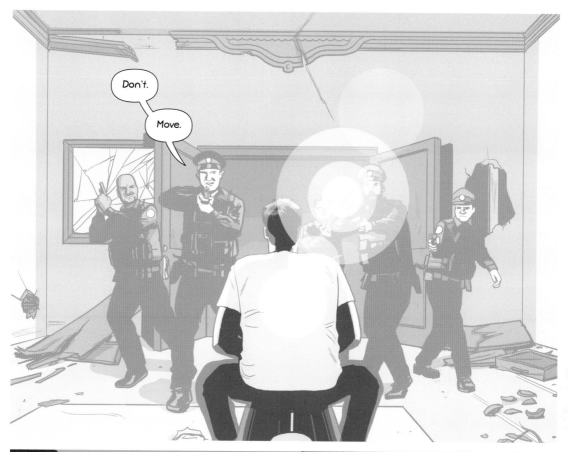

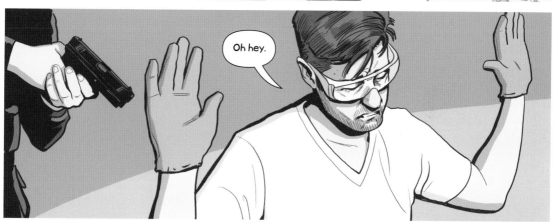

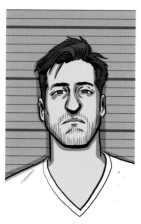 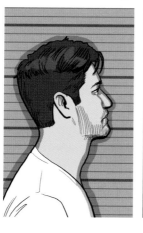

Someone asked him what he was doing.

"I wanted to see how long it would take to break everything," he said.

Nobody had the heart to tell him just how much Kuber Badal's "everything" contained.

How many other people, places, and things his tendrils grew to touch.

Because of the sheer volume of destruction, Jon was sentenced to 90 days custody, and another nine months of house arrest.

They'd let him go home in a month, assuming he wasn't a problem, behavior-wise.

And that was that.

Remove all earrings, cock rings, ball rings, butt [...] forgot about, butt plugs you were hoping we wouldn't notice, Prince Alberts and Prince Williams.

Jon went to prison.

Minimum security, but still.

He said later it was never really scary after his first day, just lonely, gross, and sad.

"Like a community college you couldn't leave," he said.

One thing he did while inside was direct some of the inmates in a stage play.

As part of their art therapy program.

He loved every minute of it, and they loved him for it.

O that this too too solid flesh would melt...

Jon found his thing.

And it would change his life.

But I'm getting ahead of myself.

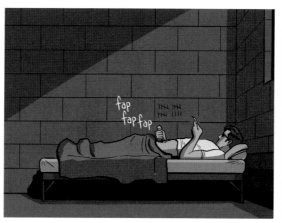

It wasn't until Jon—

Well.

fap fap fap

He couldn't see me until *he* found out the Quiet was gone.

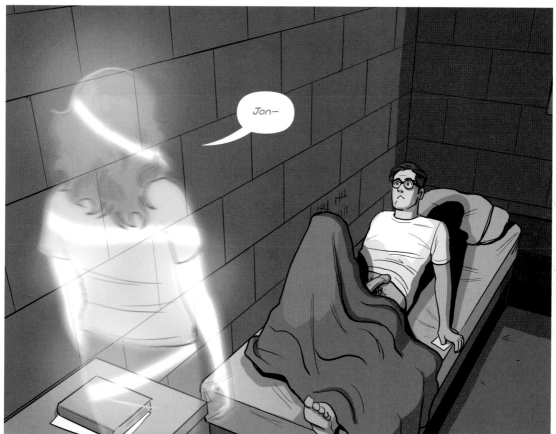

Jon—

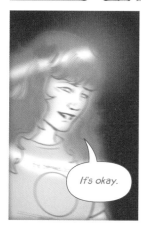

It's okay.

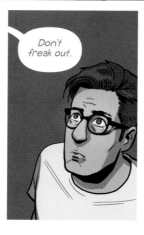

Don't freak out.

I had *found* him.

Finally.

And I could finally tell him—

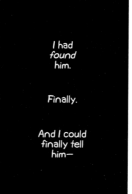

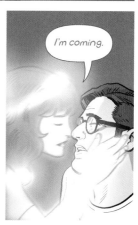

I'm coming.

30
MY BLACK HOLE

I'm not ready
for this to end.

I thought I
had more—

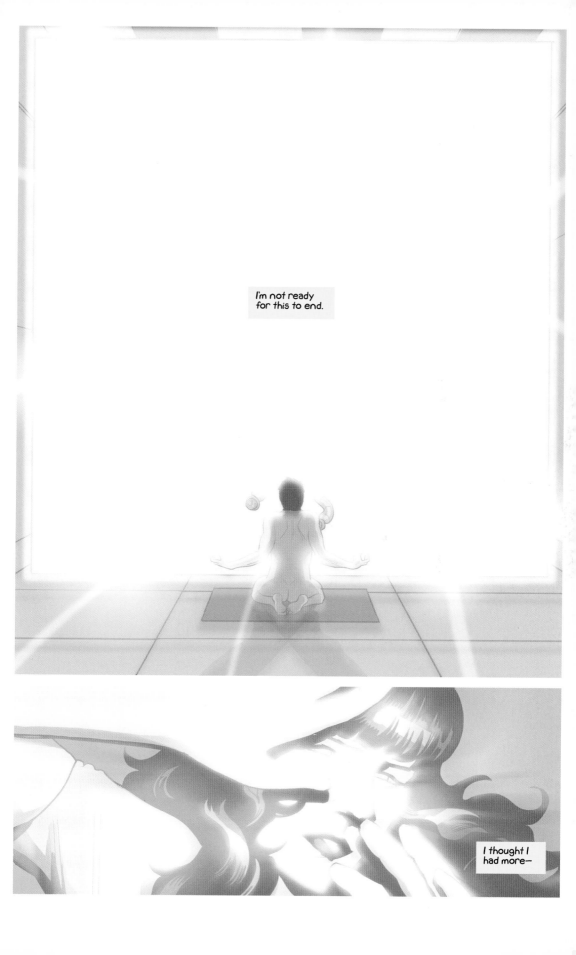

—time.
Whaaaat the...
And then...
Fuck.
I did.
In fact...

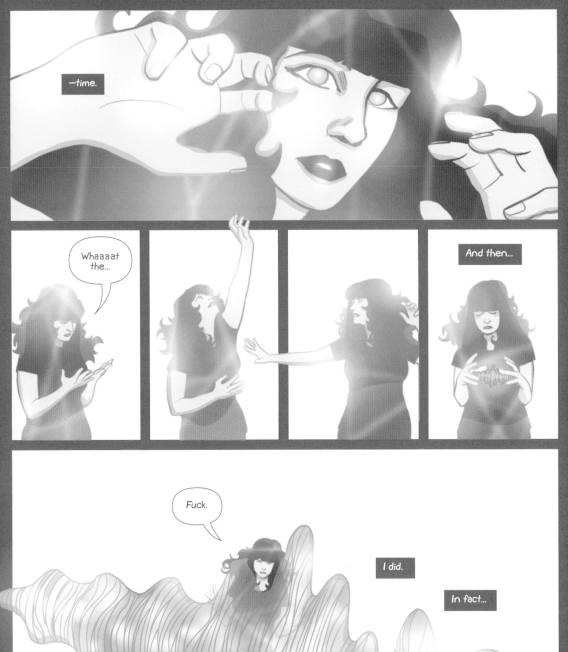

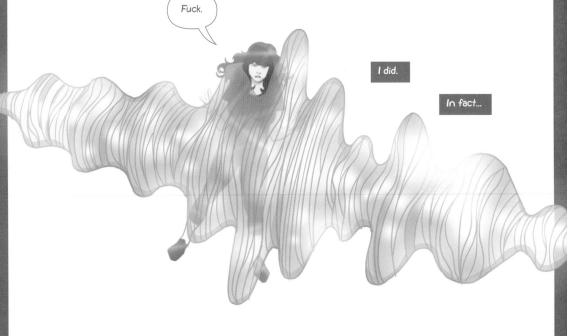

I had all the time anyone could have.

Beginning to end.

I knew I wasn't just *in* the Quiet anymore.

I was the Quiet.

I was the invisible, turbulent, constantly flowing *thing* that conjoined every moment of my life, from one to the other, start to stop.

Past and *future* were only directions here—ways I could move.

So I moved.

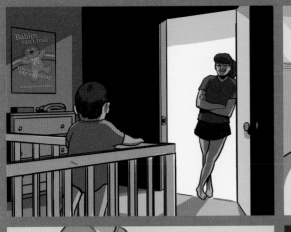

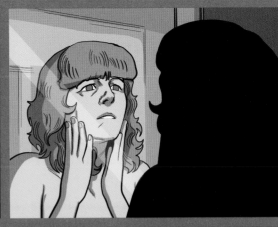

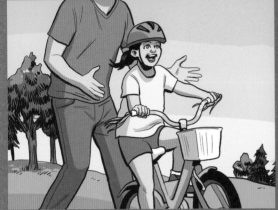

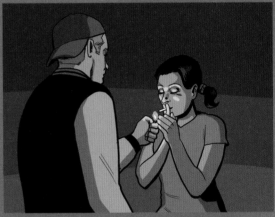

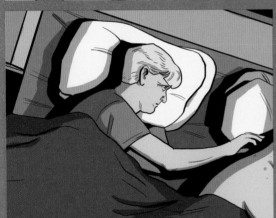

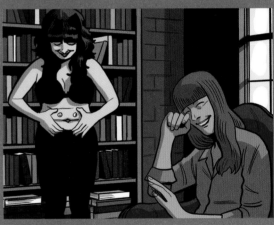

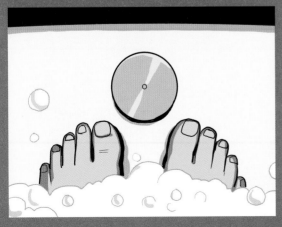

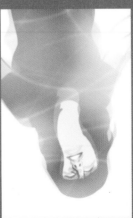

It was like my life was recorded on a filmstrip, wadded up in a ball.

And I was falling through frames, glimpsing scene after scene.

Reliving random memories—

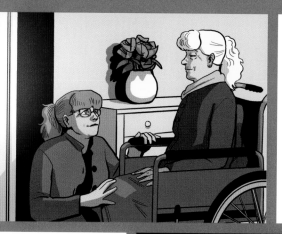

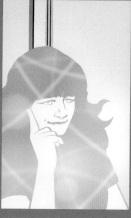

Or catching glimpses of things yet to happen.

I could feel the people in my life, the people that I love.

I could go *see* them again.

I could go back to the best times we shared.

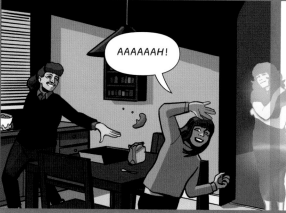

AAAAAAH!

Because they're all *here*.

Because "here" is all of me.

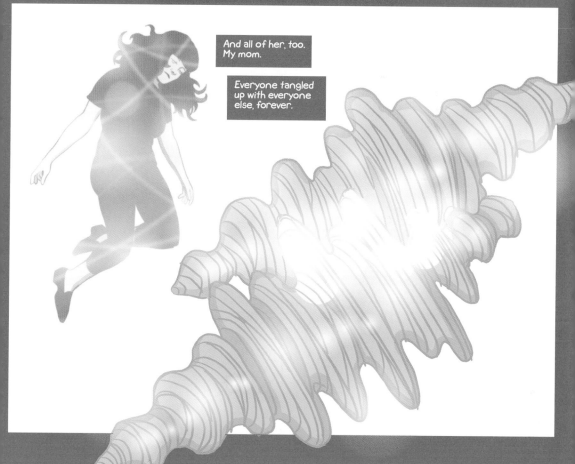

And all of her, too. My mom.

Everyone tangled up with everyone else, forever.

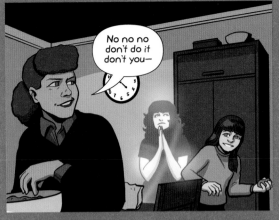

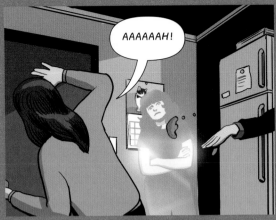

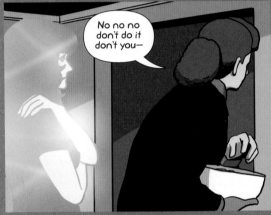

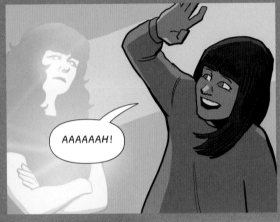

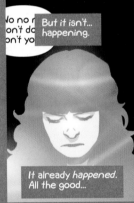

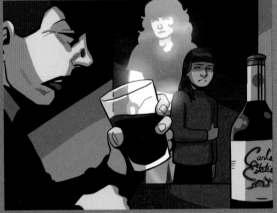

And all of
the bad.

It's real and alive as
it ever was, even in
its pastness.

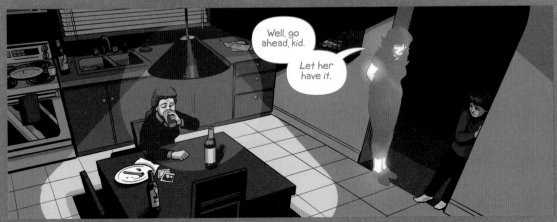

Small and heavy, like awful little magnets.
Playing out in inescapable, infinite loops.
These day-destroying, mood-killing, panic-inducing—
I don't know. Memories.
Moments.
A black hole that drags me out of whatever I'm doing...
Just to make me feel awful all over again.
The parts of the past that hold me hostage.
All the days that ruined my life.
That ruined me.
Good news, guys:
Here in Forever you can feel them all again and again.

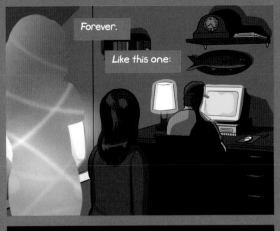

Forever.

Like this one:

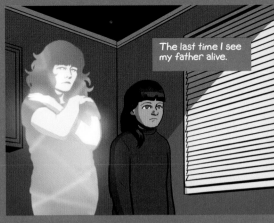

The last time I see my father alive.

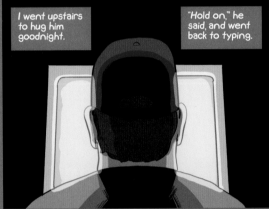

I went upstairs to hug him goodnight.

"Hold on," he said, and went back to typing.

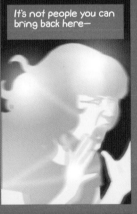

After a bit I felt ignored, so I left.

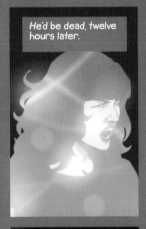

He'd be dead, twelve hours later.

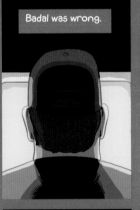

Badal was wrong.

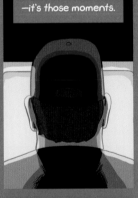

It's not people you can bring back here—

—it's those moments.

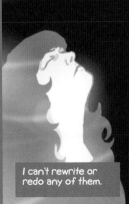

I can't rewrite or redo any of them.

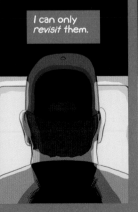

I can only *revisit* them.

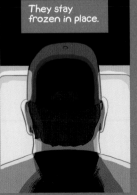

They stay frozen in place.

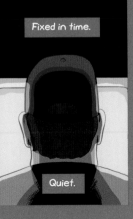

Fixed in time.

Quiet.

I feel like I'm a ghost.
And I'm haunting my own house.
Badal thought you could change those points in time...
And that would redraw the line connecting *us* to *them*.
But that line already changes.
Even if we don't feel it.
The point that starts the line stays fixed.
We are anything *but*.
As long as we're alive, anyway.

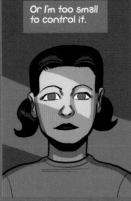

Maybe my black hole is too big to control.

Or I'm too small to control it.

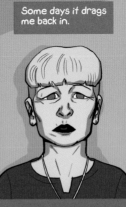

Some days it drags me back in.

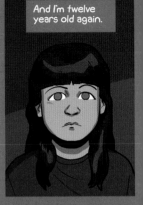

And I'm twelve years old again.

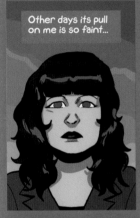

Other days its pull on me is so faint...

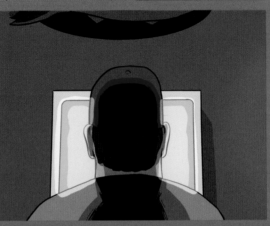

...I can't even remember his face.

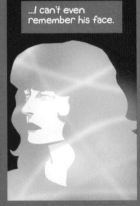

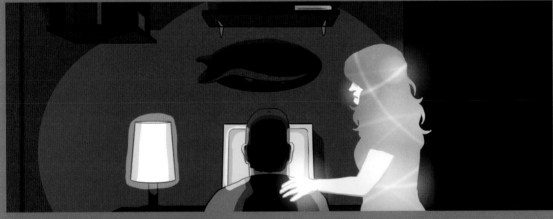

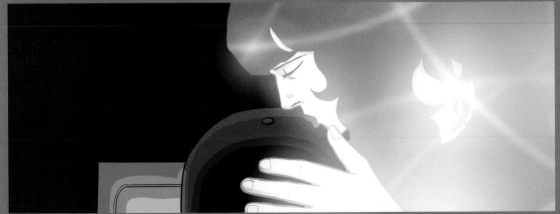

Why here? Why this, why now?
Of all the places. Of all the times.
Why did I choose to center myself in the worst of all days?
Like of all the days ever to relive, which one do you choose?
The shittiest one, obviously. Ugh.
It'd be the thing I'd change, I guess. If I could.
All these moments connect to *this* one moment.
If I changed *it*, what else would change?
Would I ever have even found the Quiet?
Would I ever have found—

Even now, bathing in the good times, I realize—
—these aren't actually good feelings—
THE BOOBY HATCH
BREAK
LET THE PROS PICK YOUR BRAIN
—these are the memories of good feelings.
CRAZY IVAN'S SMALL CARS + BIG
Maybe every trip to the Quiet was a scramble to hold onto these little moments when I could...
Well, maybe not escape the black hole...
...but forget about it.
For a while.
SAVE OUR BOOKS

To hold still, just for a second.
And be outside of it.
Memories of good times are still memories, though.
And living life like that...
Isn't being alive at all.

I can see him.
Shining in my future like a beacon.
The more he thinks about me, the brighter he gets.
I let him pull me in.
Never feeling new joy is too high a price to pay for never feeling new pain.
So maybe this is gonna hurt.
It's okay.
I can take it.
Jon—
It's okay.
Don't freak out.
I'm coming.

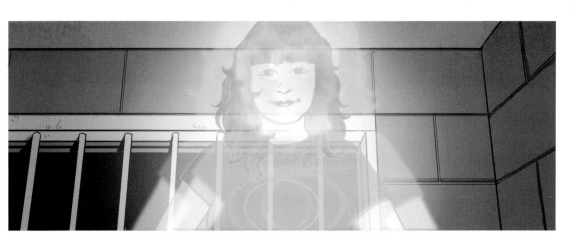

Badal's machine knocked me out of...

I don't know.

Time. Like linear, yknow, one-Mississippi, two-Mississippi—

It was like falling out of a boat.

Then waking up underwater.

Nobody ever saw Badal again.

Maybe he got his wish.

But maybe—

—unlike me—

—he didn't have anyone out there missing him.

It took *Jon* for me to find my way back.

Err—

Back-*ish.*

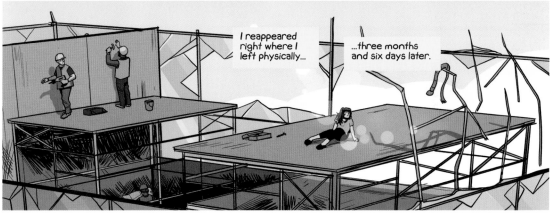

I reappeared right where I left physically...

...three months and six days later.

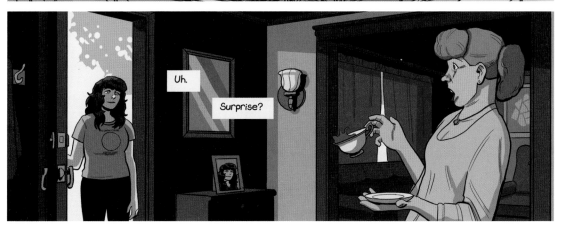

Uh.

Surprise?

There was a lot of catching up to do.

Nobody could go to the Quiet anymore but me.

The outside world assumed Badal was dead.

Jon went nuts and went to jail.

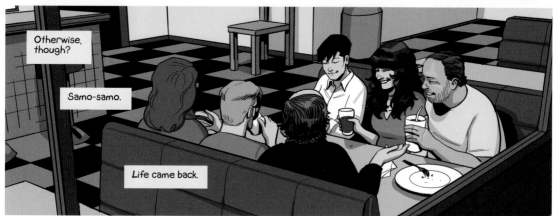

Otherwise, though?

Samo-samo.

Life came back.

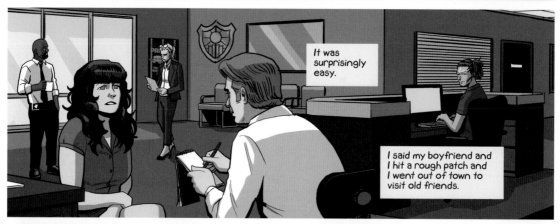

It was surprisingly easy.

I said my boyfriend and I hit a rough patch and I went out of town to visit old friends.

Since there was no proof of any crime—

— let alone accusations—

—the cops just shrugged and let me go.

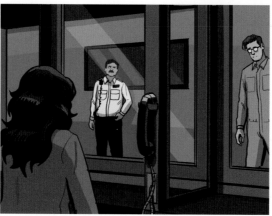

Leaving Jon holding the bag for us all.

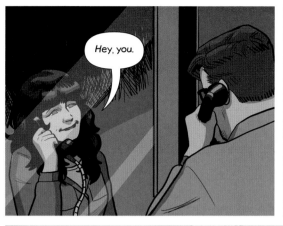

Hey, you.

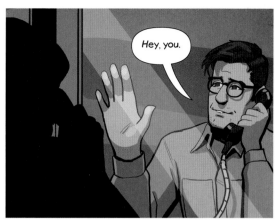

Hey, you.

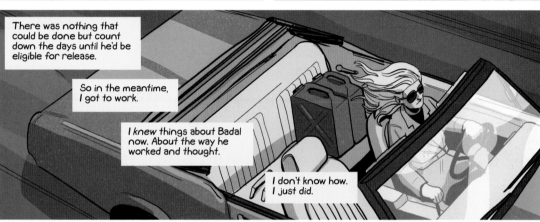

There was nothing that could be done but count down the days until he'd be eligible for release.

So in the meantime, I got to work.

I *knew* things about Badal now. About the way he worked and thought.

I don't know how. I just did.

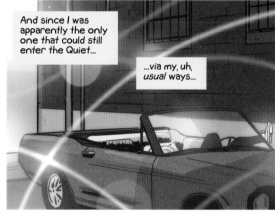

Being properly paranoid, he only kept paper records about the people like us he'd found.

How he tracked them.

How he was capturing their Quiet energy or whatever.

And since I was apparently the only one that could still enter the Quiet...

...via my, uh, *usual* ways...

I felt like it was up to me to make sure the Quiet—

—and everyone like me that he found—

—stayed secret.

And safe.

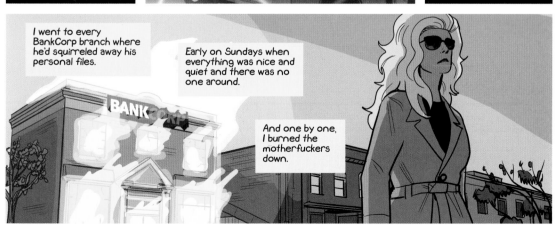

I went to every BankCorp branch where he'd squirreled away his personal files.

Early on Sundays when everything was nice and quiet and there was no one around.

And one by one, I burned the motherfuckers down.

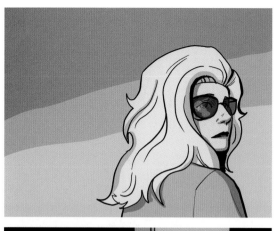

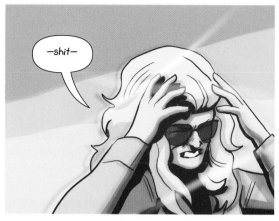

–shit–

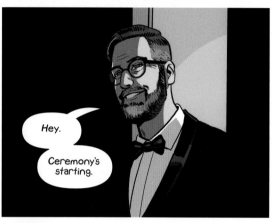

Hey.

Ceremony's starting.

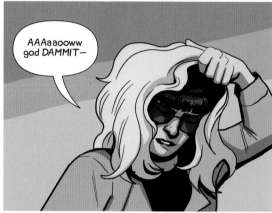

AAAaaooww god DAMMIT–

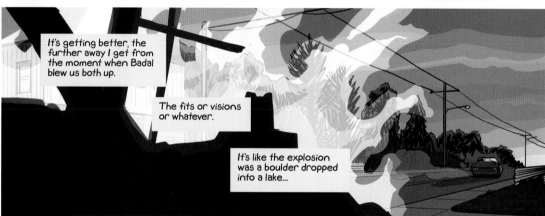

It's getting better, the further away I get from the moment when Badal blew us both up.

The fits or visions or whatever.

It's like the explosion was a boulder dropped into a lake...

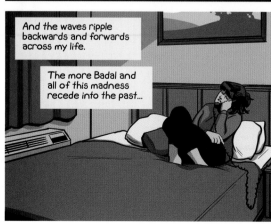

And the waves ripple backwards and forwards across my life.

The more Badal and all of this madness recede into the past...

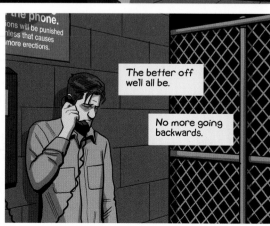

The better off we'll all be.

No more going backwards.

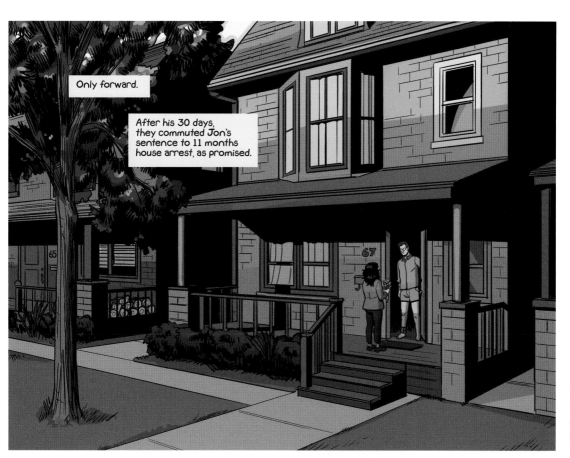

Only forward.

After his 30 days, they commuted Jon's sentence to 11 months house arrest, as promised.

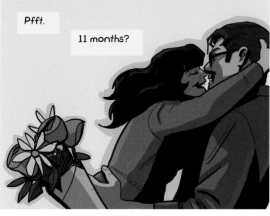

Pfft.

11 months?

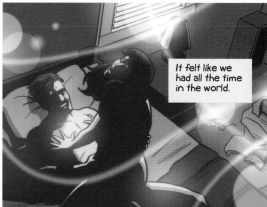

It felt like we had all the time in the world.

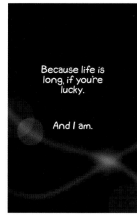

Because life is long, if you're lucky.

And I am.

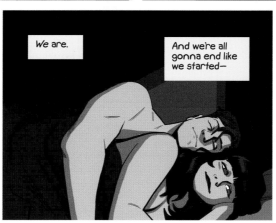

We are.

And we're all gonna end like we started—

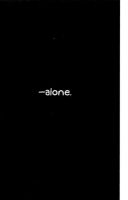

—alone.

But I know I have myself.
I know I have this moment.
And I know that this moment is really all I ever have.
I know that *in* this moment, you are here with me.
And in this moment, *we* are alone.
Together.

69
HAPPY ENDING

Hey Y'all it's
DEWEY 'n BUD'S
DESTINATION WEDDING
We're requesting the honor of your presence
Bring people if you want
We are rich now and will pay for everything
Transport, Room, Board
It is on a private
RESORT ISLAND
Like a real sweet fairytale ending
But also a dream you are having!!!! !
WE LOVE YOU
And hope to see you soon
Then all that in a pretty font
Bud + Dewey
Folks, we couldn't express the magnitude of—
—magic!—
—that's made up these last few years for us.
When we started out, we were just a couple of chums, trying to make each other laugh.
Laughter led to love, and love led to—
—well—
—this! The joy of all this!
That we have you to share in—
—any of it—
—with us is staggering and humbling. But most of all—
JOYOUS!
And now we're leaping into that joy together and making a real forever commitment to each other.
We're getting married!
ap clap clap clap clap clap clap clap clap

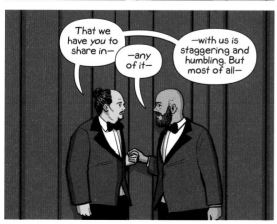

No.
No.
Babe!
No.
I'm sorry...
...but the world's gonna have to survive without any new Bud-'n-Dewey content for a little while.
I don't *care* what the network said!
Who's he?
I don't know.
Is he dangerous?
I think he's from Hollywood.
He's yelling.
A lot.
Well then fuck Steve! And fuck Marc too!
Is the whole weekend gonna be this weird?
Mm.
tink
RACHELLE RAINBOW OH MY GOD!
RAIDEN! OBERTA! LOOK IT'S YOUR AUNTIE SUZE!!

This place is—
—Unreal.
I gotta be dreaming...
Found 'em!
Keguhhh hhMyrtle!
Ms. Dickson.
Oh—
—ah—
Are we—
—uh—
Yeah okay.
You good?
Wonderful. Lovely to see you again.
I'm sorry—
—Go for Queen Bitch.
Bull*shit* it's a mercy flight.
Tell them if they violate our airspace I will *shoot them out of the sky* even if it means a torrential downpour of *child pieces* raining down on the rehearsal dinner—
Goddamn paparazzi!
Would that woman really open fire on a helicopter full of kids?
Probably.

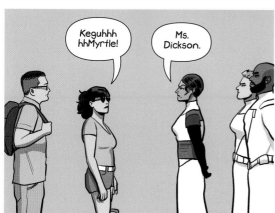

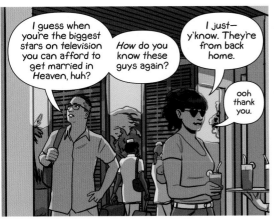

"I guess when you're the biggest stars on television you can afford to get married in Heaven, huh?"

"*How* do you know these guys again?"

"I just—y'know. They're from back home."

"ooh thank you."

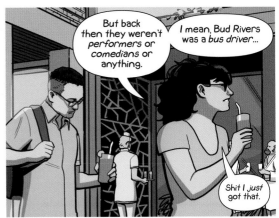

"But back then they weren't *performers* or *comedians* or anything."

"I mean, Bud Rivers was a *bus driver*..."

"Shit I *just* got that."

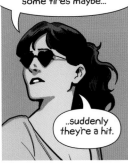

"...but, bing-bang-boom, something happens, something else happens, somebody somewhere sets some fires maybe..."

"..suddenly they're a hit."

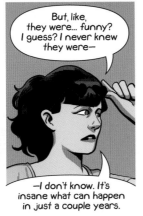

"But, like, they were... funny? I guess? I never knew they were—"

"—I don't know. It's insane what can happen in just a couple years."

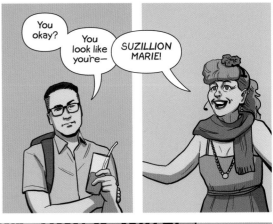

"You okay?"

"You look like you're—"

"SUZILLION MARIE!"

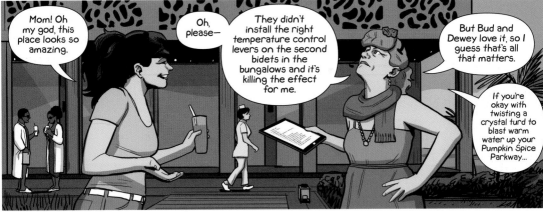

"Mom! Oh my god, this place looks so amazing."

"Oh, please—"

"They didn't install the right temperature control levers on the second bidets in the bungalows and it's killing the effect for me."

"But Bud and Dewey love it, so I guess that's all that matters."

"If you're okay with twisting a crystal turd to blast warm water up your Pumpkin Spice Parkway..."

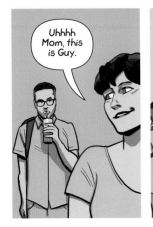

"Uhhhh Mom, this is Guy."

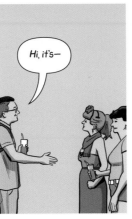

"Hi, it's—"

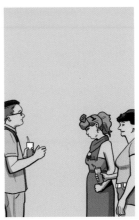

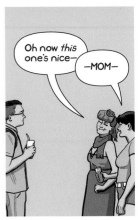

"Oh now *this* one's nice—"

"—MOM—"

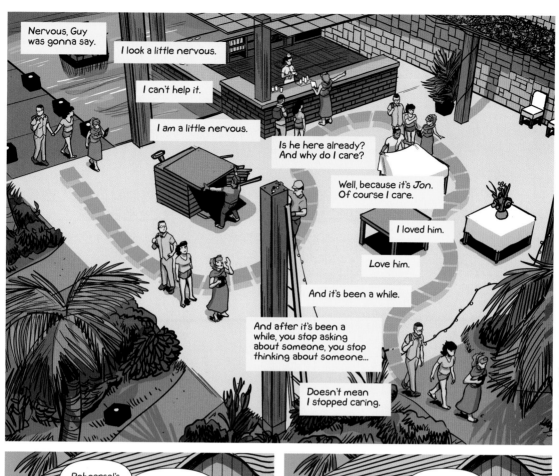

Nervous, Guy was gonna say.

I look a little nervous.

I can't help it.

I am a little nervous.

Is he here already? And why do I care?

Well, because it's *Jon*. Of course I care.

I loved him.

Love him.

And it's been a while.

And after it's been a while, you stop asking about someone, you stop thinking about someone...

Doesn't mean I stopped caring.

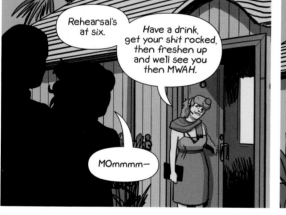

Rehearsal's at six.

Have a drink, get your shit rocked, then freshen up and we'll see you then MWAH.

MOmmmm—

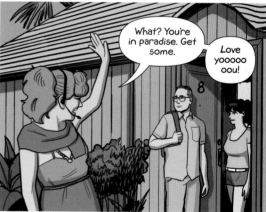

What? You're in paradise. Get some.

Love yooooo oou!

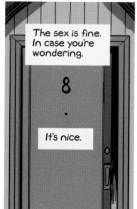

The sex is fine. In case you're wondering.

It's nice.

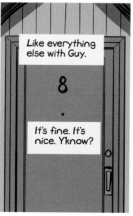

Like everything else with Guy.

It's fine. It's nice. Yknow?

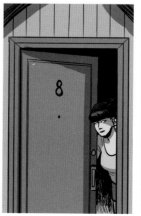

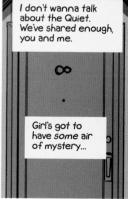

I don't wanna talk about the Quiet. We've shared enough, you and me.

Girl's got to have *some* air of mystery...

...I hope Jon's okay.
You're okay.
This is okay.
Right?
Okay.
I've shaved ballsacks smoother than that guy's flying.
Really? Why?
These two. Look at them.
I mean—they're doing great.
Well, fashion, for one.
And two, when hair is an impediment to technique, depilation increases the potential oral sex surface area some 185%.
Nothing's changed.
—Y'know what, maybe everything's changed.
It's okay.
You're here with your friends.
You're okay.
...Okay.

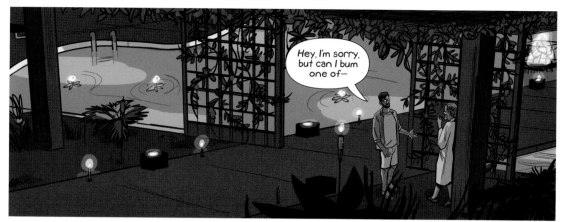

Hey, I'm sorry, but can I bum one of—

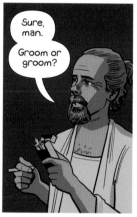

Sure, man.

Groom or groom?

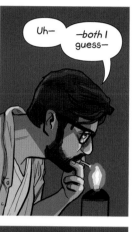

Uh— —both I guess—

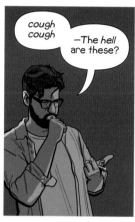

cough cough

—The *hell* are these?

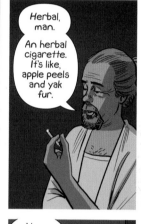

Herbal, man.

An herbal cigarette. It's like, apple peels and yak fur.

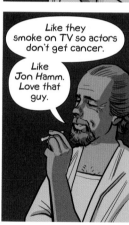

Like they smoke on TV so actors don't get cancer.

Like Jon Hamm. Love that guy.

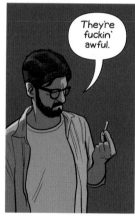

They're fuckin' awful.

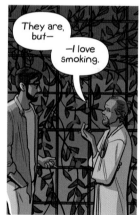

They are, but— —I love smoking.

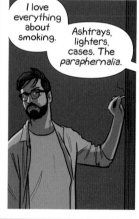

I love everything about smoking.

Ashtrays, lighters, cases. The paraphernalia.

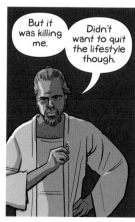

But it was killing me.

Didn't want to quit the lifestyle though.

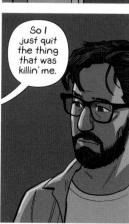

So I just quit the thing that was killin' me.

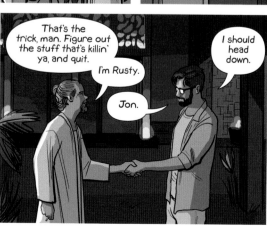

That's the trick, man. Figure out the stuff that's killin' ya, and quit.

I'm Rusty.

Jon.

I should head down.

What am I afraid of?
Here, in this place, surrounded by all of these friends with their joy and laughter and good-ness.
That I'm going to lose it?
That *she's* going to lose it?
Lose what? Why?
We split.
It was amicable. Sometimes things don't work out.
What can you do?
Oohhh, wait.
Now I know what I'm afraid of.
I'm afraid it's going to hurt.
But...
...it's good.
She looks good.
He looks good.
Older.

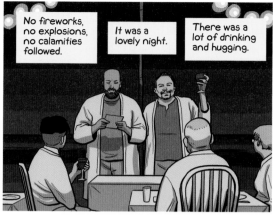

No fireworks, no explosions, no calamities followed.

It was a lovely night.

There was a lot of drinking and hugging.

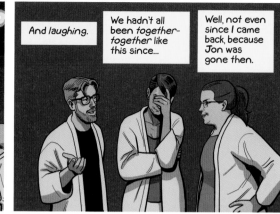

And *laughing*.

We hadn't all been *together-together* like this since...

Well, not even since I came back, because Jon was gone then.

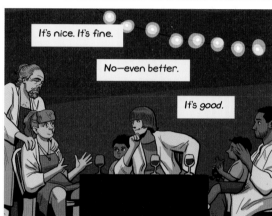

It's nice. It's fine.

No—even better.

It's *good*.

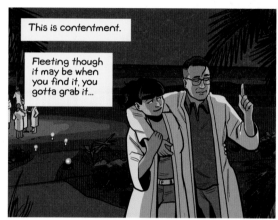

This is contentment.

Fleeting though it may be when you find it, you gotta grab it...

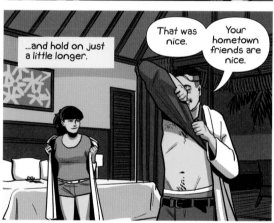

...and hold on just a little longer.

That was nice.

Your hometown friends are nice.

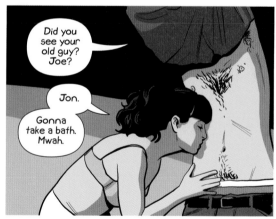

Did you see your old guy? Joe?

Jon.

Gonna take a bath. Mwah.

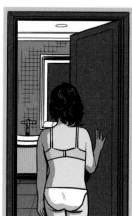

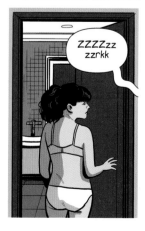

ZZZZzz zzrkk

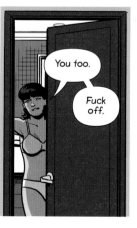

You too.

Fuck off.

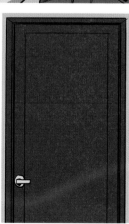

KOOMKOOMKOOM
EAT 23 MILLIMETERS OF MY MOLTEN HOT LEAD DICK-MISSILES PAPARAZZO SCUM!
KOOMKOOM
Ooph, that's loud.
Kegelface told me those are real anti-aircraft guns.
Who?
ZEENTHORKE CARES
Oh. Uh. She—
The uh—
We used to—
Myrtle. The security ladOOPH
Excuse me I am so sor—
—oh.

Hey, you!
Hey!
Hey you.
Hey, you.
—mess I made—
—Please, this is hardly one of my *archival* heirloom t-shirts with words—
—sorry we didn't get a chance to—
—please, no, everyone was having so much fun—
—wasn't it fun? Everybody together?
So much fun. Hey I'm Jon.
Oh. Uh. Guy. Hi.
Doin' okay there, Guy?
Little dehydrated maybe.
You wanna join us, or—
Here we go.
—Sure! Great.
Here we go.

Suze says you're a teacher?
Yeah a... quasi-social worker-slash-teacher, I guess.
I work with a program that brings the arts into the prison system, and then provides art therapy on the other side.
FLORAL PRINT
Really? That's—wow, how does one come to that?
Well, one does a little time, as I did, and comes out on the other side pretty changed.
FLORAL
I was pretty...
adrift when I went in.
But while I was in, I really found...
...well, "calling" sounds cheesy, but a thing I love doing.
Can I ask—
Can I ask what you did?
Guy, no c'mon—
Basic problems-with-authority stuff.
Pooped in plants.
Robbed some banks.
Destroyed a mansion or whatever.
Ha.
That's funny.
Anyway, when this one went back to school for her doctorate, I decided to help people the way I needed help.
PRINT
Wow. So the guy with the problem with authority grows up to become a teacher, how 'bout that.
Irony's a real motherfucker sometimes, huh?
FLORAL PRINT

Dearly beloved—
Gathered family, friends both new and old—
Children, beautiful and innocent—
Strangers and background characters, all surely starring in the unique stories of your own rich lives—
The journey of life is long, if you're lucky. And I think we can agree, we are, all of us, in our ways lucky.
Life can be long and hard, and sometimes mean and cold, and there is nothing more painful than navigating that path alone.
And so to find someone—
—to help, to trust, to treasure—
—to want, and need, and desire—
To love.
...Is truly a reason to celebrate and be grateful.
And so we have gathered here to celebrate the marriage of these two beautiful souls forged separately in their own struggles, but now—
Conjoined on their journey.
Not alone but together.
And together they summoned us, not simply to bear witness—
—but so that they may testify of their love for one another before us all, and celebrate with gratitude all who made such a union, and such a journey possible.
Weddings are both ending of one and one—
—and the beginning of two.
The alignment of stars, friends, that must form to make days like today possible is nothing short of miraculous.
They're lucky, each and every one, and should be treasured.
And so we thank you, all of you, boundlessly and endlessly for joining us at this ending.
And at this beginning.
Bud...?

"Dewey, you make—"
sigh
This is no good.
I—you—
Oh my *god*, you make me laugh, dude.
And, I mean—I know I laugh a little at *everything*.
But only just a little.
You make me laugh a *lot*.
You make me happy-laugh. And that's really hard.
Because you get me. And I think—
—I hope—
—*I know* I get you, too.
I get that you are kind and good and compassionate.
That's super-duper rare out there, man.
And I know, the more time I spend with you, the more kind and good and compassionate I am.
You're just awesome.
And all these people, all our friends that came all this way with us—just super-super awesome.
I love you. Will you be my husband?

I will.
And Bud—
You've been here for me through so much these last few years.
All these transformations, these things that felt so impossible to survive, understand, endure—
The worst days of my life.
Days when I hated who I was, what was inside of me; days when I thought I'd come apart, but you—
You were there.
You were always there.
You never flinched.
Or judged.
You wanted to *help*.
I don't know how to say thank you for that, but with your kind permission, I would like to spend the rest of my life trying.
Dang.
Will you be *my* husband?
Yes. I will.
By the powers vested in me, the Cosmic QuantiPope, by the Infinilactic Crystal Goddess of Love...

I hereby decree across the known universe—
You are not two, you are one.
Married.
And just like that...
Two become one.
They made it look like the easiest thing in the world.
But it's not.

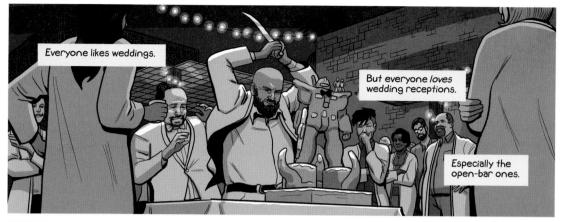

Everyone likes weddings.

But everyone *loves* wedding receptions.

Especially the open-bar ones.

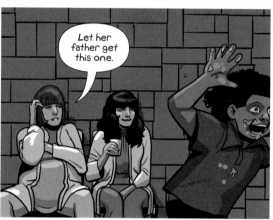

Let her father get this one.

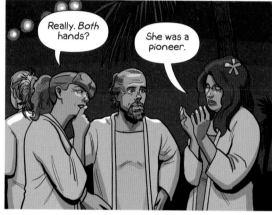

Really. *Both* hands?

She was a pioneer.

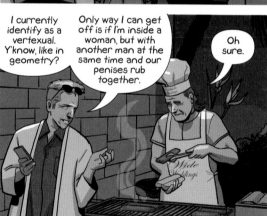

I currently identify as a vertexual. Y'know, like in geometry?

Only way I can get off is if I'm inside a woman, but with another man at the same time and our penises rub together.

Oh sure.

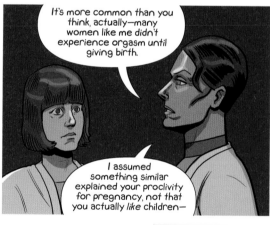

It's more common than you think, actually—many women like me didn't experience orgasm until giving birth.

I assumed something similar explained your proclivity for pregnancy, not that you actually *like* children—

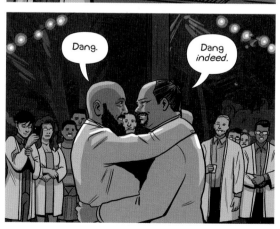

Dang.

Dang *indeed.*

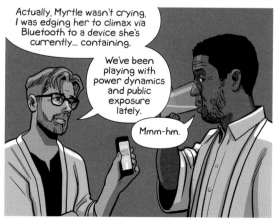

Actually, Myrtle wasn't crying, I was edging her to climax via Bluetooth to a device she's currently... containing.

We've been playing with power dynamics and public exposure lately.

Mmm-hm.

It's both our favorites on the inside, chocolate *and* vanilla!
You're never touching me again.
Deal.
Far *out*, man.
It was a lovely day.
It really was, and I'm glad you were here for it.
Mom, is this a cult? The robes, the pope hat, the "Crystal Goddess of Love"?
Oh, praise Zeenthorke no—it's a *psychodynamic* way of living.
CABIN 10-24
WASHROOMS
ANTI-AIRCRAFT GUN
It starts, before you even notice.
The beginning of the end.
Okay, little one, time for bed...

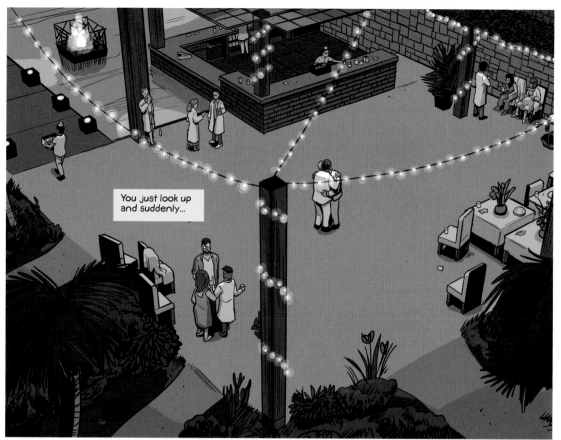

You just look up and suddenly...

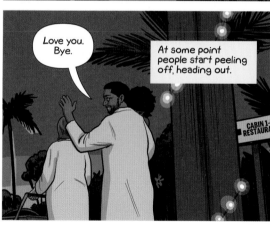

Love you. Bye.

At some point people start peeling off, heading out.

CABIN 1-(
RESTAURA

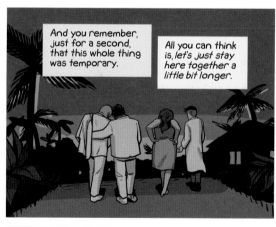

And you remember, just for a second, that this whole thing was temporary.

All you can think is, *let's just stay here together a little bit longer.*

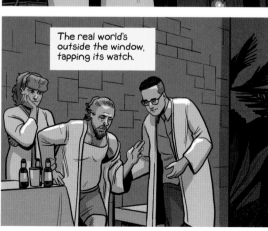

The real world's outside the window, tapping its watch.

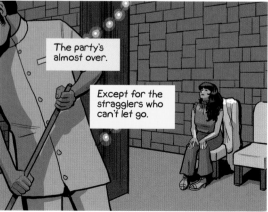

The party's almost over.

Except for the stragglers who can't let go.

Not yet, anyway.
Hey you.
Hey you.
Never actually saw the sun rise over the ocean before.
It's pretty good.

Yeah, it's okay.
How are you?
I'm... okay.
Okay enough?
Contentish? Lucky. Right now? It's enough.
How are you?
I'm fine. It's fine.
School is a lot. And he's nice. It's okay.
Everything's okay.
I'm so close to my doctorate, I kind of don't have room for thunder and drama all the time, y'know?
He doesn't—
There's no thunder.
No lightning, either.
Well.
Not everyone is like you.
Not everyone is like us.
Eh. Life is long.
We should probably head out.

Yeah. We should, but...
...let's stay here together.
Just a little bit more.
Okay?

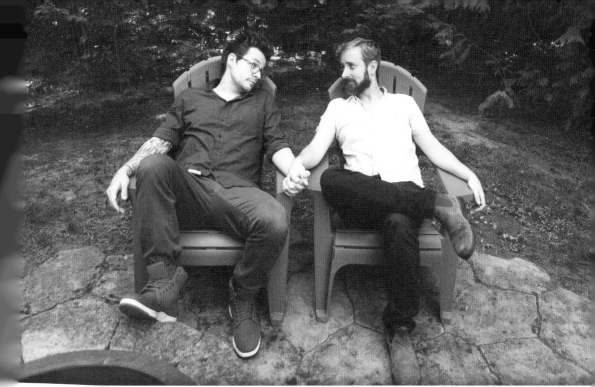

Photo by Ed Peterson

Well folks, we've finally made it... the halfway point! Just kidding, we're fucking cooked. This whole thing would've only been a joke that made me and Chip laugh and lose money without the insane, glorious, wonderful, hilarious, honest, fearless, rabid, and quite frankly horned-up readers who took to *Sex Criminals* with the zeal of a sexy crusader with the disposable income of 18-35 year olds who also like dick jokes.

You changed our lives, our careers, and our understanding of just how lame literally every other audience or readership is in comparison. My time writing *Sex Criminals* has ruined me for anything else; because of you this will always be my professional high-water mark.

Chip honey can you pick up some more Cheez-Its on the way home Daddy hungy

A lot of people throw around the phrase "life-changing" willy-nilly. I know I do it. I actually just had a life-changing sandwich for lunch. But nothing comes close to actually being life-changing quite like Matt and me deciding to make a fun, dirty comic together that we anticipated no one ever wanting besides us.

Now, seven years later, we're wrapping up our story that took us across the world, put us on all sorts of (good) lists, and turned us from "online friends" into lifelong best friends.

I'll forever be grateful to those of you who joined us for this ride, but, and I feel bad saying this, I never drew the book for you. I drew it for Matt. To surprise him when I could, to hopefully add something to his already remarkable words, and, most importantly, to make my friend laugh.

Thanks for everything.

Matt Fraction wrote
Sex Criminals.

Chip Zdarsky drew
Sex Criminals.

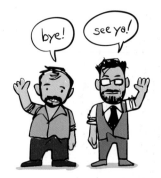